LOOKING BACK AT BRITAIN

FLOWER POWER TO UNION POWER

1970s

LOOKING BACK AT BRITAIN

FLOWER POWER TO UNION POWER

1970s

James Harpur

Reader's Digest | gettyimages

CONTENTS

1970s IMAGE GALLERY
FRONT COVER: The groom sported fashionable sideburns while the bride dressed in suede hot-pants and thigh-length boots for their wedding at Kensington Register Office in 1971.
BACK COVER: A little girl bounces on a space-hopper, the very latest in trendy toys, in the summer of 1971. She is modelling clothes from the new children's range for the Littlewoods winter catalogue.
TITLE PAGE: A gang of young girls playing in a narrow urban alley in 1970.
OPPOSITE: A view of Wentworth Street Market in Aldgate, including Max Chessi, the oldest stallholder, in 1978.
FOLLOWING PAGES:
A young mother and child at the Hyde Park Festival in July 1970.
A policeman joins in the fun at Notting Hill carnival in 1978.
A group of leather-clad Punks, ahead of their time in the early 1970s.
The Queen greets well-wishers on a walkabout during the Silver Jubilee celebrations in 1977.

GROWING
DISSATISFACTION

For many Britons, the Seventies began as a seamless extension of the Sixties. Flower power may have started to wane, but there were still plenty of petals left to drop. And yet something was changing. Despite almost full employment, the nation's workforce was restless and discontented. At times, the decade seemed like one long arm-wrestle between the government and the unions.

POLICE AND PICKETS   A striker is arrested at the Saltley Coke Depot in Birmingham in February 1972. Some 15,000 miners had formed a mass picket at the depot, which the police struggled to contain.

A CHANGE OF LEADERSHIP

The decade began with Harold Wilson and the Labour Party in power at Westminster. The economy was fragile. The Vietnam War dragged on, as did protests against it, even though Britain was not directly involved. English football was still riding high after the heroics of 1966. People went to pubs not to watch sport on Sky but to play darts, while smoking Embassy Filters and Player's No.6, drinking pints of Watney's Red Barrel and Worthington 'E' – then they drove home tipsy without wearing a seat-belt. On television *Coronation Street* was going strong, as was *Dad's Army, Dr Who, Crossroads* and *Blue Peter*. Flared trousers, cheesecloth shirts and long hair seemed ubiquitous. Young people tuned in to Johnny Walker, Tony Blackburn and John Peel on Radio 1 for the latest music, and some turned on with marijuana.

For the government, the industrial unrest that figured large in the late Sixties remained a major issue. In January 1969 Secretary of Employment Barbara Castle had published a White Paper, *In Place of Strife,* that aimed to curb unofficial strikes and ameliorate industrial relations. But the Trades Union Congress (TUC), along with influential voices among Labour backbenchers, and even in the Cabinet, set their faces against it. By June, Wilson was forced to climb down and appeal to the TUC's better nature rather than imposing legislation. The TUC gave its 'solemn and binding' agreement that it would cooperate with the government, and Wilson presented this as a substantial concession. But he was fooling nobody: the *Economist* referred to it as a TUC victory 'In Place of Government', while 'Solomon Binding' became a national joke character, epitomising TUC promises. Labour's failure to grasp the nettle of trade union reform would return time and again to haunt them – and the country – throughout the decade.

> 'In British politics the seventies began as they would go on: with a shallow feeling of optimism followed by a jolt.'
>
> Andy Beckett, from *When the Lights Went Out: Britain in the Seventies*

Despite this setback, Labour rallied during the first half of 1970. The balance of payments was improving under Chancellor Roy Jenkins. Opinion polls were going Labour's way. And there was the prospect of another football world cup that year in Mexico, promoting a benign mood of anticipation – a chirpy Harold Wilson quipped that England always won a world cup under a Labour government. On 18 May Wilson felt confident enough to call an election for 18 June.

The Conservatives, under Edward (Ted) Heath, were ready for an electoral fight. In January they had begun the new decade by planning a right-wing programme at a conference at the Selsdon Park Hotel in Croydon. This included trade union reform, lower taxation and some privatisation of nationalised

LIKELY LADS
Posterity may have labelled it the decade that fashion forgot, but at the time bomber jackets, flared trousers and chunky platform shoes were pretty cool. These teenagers in Deptford in January 1973 are typical of a style that emerged as hippie headbands, scarves and beads disappeared. Harrington jackets, Ben Sherman shirts and ex-army greatcoats were all in demand. Unofficial murals and graffiti became a common sight, especially in run-down areas. The poster on the door (top right) is advertising the Albany Empire, an old Deptford institution that supported Rock Against Racism when it emerged later in the decade. The venue was destroyed by fire in 1978 and officially reopened by Princess Diana in 1982.

industries. Wilson referred waspishly to 'Selsdon Man', as if he were a paleolithic right-winger. But there was nothing stone age about the Tories' organisation. They were in good shape at grassroots level and although the influential Tory maverick, Enoch Powell, was attacking Heath on a range of issues, from tax cuts to policies on Northern Ireland, they had everything to play for.

Rivals for power

The election was a two-way contest between old rivals Harold Wilson and Edward Heath. The Liberal leader Jeremy Thorpe, a flamboyant Old Etonian who cut a dash in his trilby hats and silk waistcoats, was still striving to convince the public of his gravitas. During the campaign the media focused sharply on the personalities of the two leading players. Both were born in 1916, came from similar grammar school backgrounds, went up to Oxford University and had worked hard to gain their position and the respect of their peers. Heath had little popular appeal – his hobbies of sailing yachts and conducting music seemed elitist and he came across as stiff and brittle, a decent 'facts-and-figures' man rather than a hand-shaker. But Wilson was faring no better in the public's affections. The old campaigner was a more accomplished television performer than his opponent, and his one-liners were more telling than Heath's, but he was commonly perceived as wily and manipulative, a pragmatic fixer rather than a principled statesman.

THREE LEADERS
Jeremy Thorpe (left), Harold Wilson (centre) and Edward Heath (right) – leaders respectively of the Liberal, Labour and Tory parties – photographed in November 1970 at a ceremony to mark the 25th anniversary of the United Nations. In the 1970 election the witty and assured Wilson was far more telegenic than the more formal and humourless Heath. Heath did manage to crack a joke when Wilson was hit by an egg, saying that people carried eggs on the off chance they might bump into the Prime Minister. Wilson parried that eggs must be cheap enough to throw about, but if the Tories got in, 'in five years no-one will be able to afford to buy an egg'. The election saw plenty of negative campaigning: this Labour poster (right) caricatures the Conservatives – from left to right, Iain Macleod, Enoch Powell, Edward Heath, Reginald Maudling, Quintin Hogg and Alec Douglas-Home – as Yesterday's Men.

Mike Yarwood, the star impersonator of the day, turned the pair into a comedy double act on his television show, depicting Wilson in avuncular, 'I-know-best', pipe-smoking cosiness and Heath with shaking shoulders whenever he broke out into a mirthless, toothy laugh. In typical forthright fashion Enoch Powell, reacting to the media obsession with the two leaders, asked rhetorically whether the election was simply between a man with a boat and a man with a pipe.

The World Cup and the election

At first it looked as if Wilson's confidence was justified, with polls remaining in Labour's favour. The late spring weather was warm and dry, and football fans were relishing the World Cup – the first to be broadcast in colour in the UK – which kicked off on 31 May. England, as holders, were one of the favourites. Their biggest initial hurdle was Brazil, who were drawn in the same group. The match between the kings of South American football and the cup holders was acclaimed as one of the great games in soccer history, even though it ended in what appears to be a boring scoreline – Brazil just shaded it to win 1-0.

Despite the setback, England still qualified for the quarter finals, to be played on 14 June, just five days before the election. They had every confidence of going further, even though their opponents were the old enemy, West Germany. Before the match first-choice goalkeeper Gordon Banks went down with food poisoning, but England coasted comfortably into a 2-0 lead. Then things unravelled. Some

FOOTBALL WIVES IN THE SEVENTIES
Some 30 years before the term 'Wags' was coined, four of England's football wives – from left to right, Kathy Peters, Judith Hurst, Tina Moore and Frances Bonetti – cheer on the team at the start of England's opening World Cup match against Romania in Mexico on 2 June, 1970. England won 1-0 and had high hopes of retaining the Jules Rimet trophy. The spine of the 1966 winning team was still intact, with the two Bobbys – Moore and Charlton – and Gordon Banks still stars on the world stage. In the event, England went out in the quarter finals, but not before playing an unforgettable match against Brazil – a superb spectacle of skilful, open football. Brazil had one of the greatest attacking line-ups of all time, with Pelé, Jairzinho, Rivelino, Cesar and Tostao all capable of shredding defences at will. England had their chances, but Brazil, through Jairzinho, took theirs. Banks made an extraordinary diving save of a Pelé header to keep the score to a creditable 1-0. Brazil went on to win the tournament.

TRUE BLUE WOMEN

Ten days after his election victory, Edward Heath parades for the cameras outside the House of Commons with 13 of the 15 elected Conservative women MPs. Second from the right is Margaret Thatcher, later to become Heath's nemesis. At the time this was a record number of women MPs for a political party at Westminster. Ten women MPs were returned for Labour at the same election. Despite the energy and rhetoric of the feminist movement – and with the singular exception of Mrs Thatcher – the Seventies was not a breakthrough decade for women politicians. There were three more elections in the decade – two in 1974 and one in 1979 – which returned respectively 23, 27 and 19 women MPs in total across all parties. The number of women MPs would not increase significantly until the 1990s, in particular 1997 when 101 Labour women – the so-called 'Blair's Babes' – won seats.

30 million fans watched anxiously as the Germans pulled a goal back. Confidence and energy was visibly draining from the England legs. Germany equalised then, in extra time, Gerd Müller scored the winner.

It is hard to know how much the sense of disappointment, even despondency, affected the election. But as with the England football team, Labour unravelled towards the end of the electoral game. Bad news about inflation and the balance of payments dampened the government's campaign. Then Enoch Powell, late in the day, voiced his support for Heath. The Tories won by 330 seats to Labour's 288. The Liberals had a disaster, losing half their seats to be left with just six. Labour and Tories joked that the parliamentary Liberal Party could fit into a taxi – after the election of Cyril Smith in 1972 the joke was amended to two taxis.

'... the new Conservative government under Edward Heath ... made a last effort to bludgeon Britain into a bigger, brighter, more "efficient" future ...'

Christopher Booker, from *The Seventies*

More than half a million people spread themselves out on the fields of East Afton Farm (left), creating a shanty town of tents focused on the stage – the artist performing here (bottom left) is Ralph McTell. The event was blessed with good weather and people could cool off and clean up with a swim at the beach (below), but the influx put huge strain on the Isle of Wight's infrastructure. Festival facilities struggled to cope, with not enough food or toilets, but there was a medical tent for those who overdosed on sun or LSD; there was relatively little in the way of alcohol. Hell's Angels were a threatening presence, and at one point fans broke down the site fence to watch the bands for free, but for an event of its magnitude it was remarkably trouble free.

FESTIVAL FREEDOM

Flower power was still going strong in the early 1970s, and nowhere was this more evident than at rock festivals like the Isle of Wight and Glastonbury. The event staged on Afton Down on the Isle of Wight in the summer of 1970 was Britain's Woodstock. It attracted 600,000 people – hippies, students, music fans – who packed onto the small ferries leaving the mainland to enjoy a five-day feast of music and fun in the open air. Topping the bill were the likes of Jimi Hendrix, The Doors, The Who, Jethro Tull and the newly formed Emerson, Lake and Palmer. And all this for a ticket costing just £3.

A SHOW OF STARS

The Isle of Wight festival attracted some of the genuine greats of rock and folk music. Jimi Hendrix took the stage in the early hours of the morning and, despite some technical problems, produced a storming set that included his majestic anti-war song, 'Machine Gun'. It was Hendrix's last UK appearance. He died in London just a couple of weeks later – on 18 September, 1970 – having choked in his sleep after too much drink and drugs. Rock fans all over the world mourned his loss. Jethro Tull performed their own unique brand of folk-rock. Their lead singer and flautist Ian Anderson (above right) cavorted enthusiastically around the stage, often adopting his performance party trick of playing on one leg, yoga-style. Other big names on the bill included two of Canada's finest singer-songwriters, Leonard Cohen (right) and Joni Mitchell (far right). Cohen, who was 35 at the time of the festival, delighted his many fans with his hit 'Suzanne'. Mitchell, in a long yolk-yellow dress, received a standing ovation for her 'Big Yellow Taxi'.

GREAT PYRAMID
The Glastonbury festival was first staged in 1970, when it was called the Pilton Festival. The following year it was renamed Glastonbury Fayre and featured the first incarnation of the pyramid stage (left), made from metal sheets mounted on scaffolding. The structure of the pyramid was supposed to mimic the proportions of the Great Pyramid of Giza and to channel Earth energies, a mystical philosophy inspired by John Michell's cult book *The View over Atlantis*, published in 1969. The 1971 Fayre starred acts such as David Bowie – not yet the superstar he would become a few years later – Family, Traffic, Fairport Convention and Melanie. The weather was as good as the music and about 7,000 people turned up to enjoy it – a small showing, perhaps, but it was the start of something big. In the 40 years since, Glastonbury has grown into the world's most celebrated open-air music festival, featuring hundreds of acts – some 700 in 2007 – and attracting an audience of up to 200,000 people.

THE TORIES TESTED

NOT WAVING, BUT VOTING
Workers raise their hands to vote on 31 July, 1970, in response to the shop steward's call to support striking workers at British Leyland. The greatest problem facing the Heath government was how to tackle the power of the unions. The 'show of hands' – which was clearly open to interpretation, not to mention possible intimidation – seemed to many to be symptomatic of the cavalier way that unions conducted their affairs. Robert Carr, the new Conservative Employment Secretary, tried to get to grips with unofficial strikes through his Industrial Relations Act, which was passed in 1971. But the Act proved ineffectual and union power remained formidable throughout the decade.

As the new Conservative Prime Minister, Ted Heath soon felt the force of the unions, of which there were more than 600 in the country at the time. The dockers went on strike in July, forcing the Home Secretary, Reginald Maudling, to call a state of emergency – the first of five during Heath's troubled premiership. Then, in autumn, industrial action was taken by the refuse collectors and sewage workers, swiftly followed by the power workers, which led to electricity cuts.

An ongoing problem for the Conservative government was convincing the public of its ability to govern. In comparison to Labour's shadow cabinet, Heath's team in general lacked charisma and leadership qualities. Heath was further hampered by the loss of two of his most able generals. His Chancellor, the talented Iain Macleod, died of a heart attack in July 1970, and Reginald Maudling, another intellectual heavyweight, was to resign in the summer of 1972 because of his connection with a financial scandal involving the architect John Poulson. Macleod's replacement, Anthony Barber, failed to inspire public confidence. His strategy was to promote growth through cutting taxes and relaxing the lending limits for the banks – in effect, a borrower's charter. Both inflation and unemployment started to rise and a new economic term, 'stagflation' – actually coined by Macleod back in 1965 – came into use.

The Tories introduced a new Industrial Relations Bill, which became law in August 1971. The new Act gave the unions new rights but in return required ballots before calling a strike, along with other measures. It was, in effect, a close cousin of Barbara Castle's failed White Paper, *In Place of Strife*. Predictably, the unions were going to object no less adamantly to a Tory attempt to curb their power than to a Labour one. But before that could happen, another Conservative principle was tested to breaking point. The government had come to power

RUBBISH PARKING
'The unions were an estate of the realm with whom cooperation was both desirable and necessary, if the nation was to remain united.' So wrote Ted Heath in his memoirs, paying due respect to the organisations that before long would cripple then sink his regime. Jack Jones, the general secretary of the TGWU in the 1970s, returned the compliment, crediting Heath for his efforts at forging a rapport with the unions. But the onslaught of strikes faced by the Tory Prime Minister was relentless. The one staged by council refuse collectors in the autumn of 1970 was particularly unsavoury, resulting in piles of rubbish accumulating in city streets, as here in Hoxton Square in London.

trumpeting the principle of non-intervention in industry. But Rolls-Royce, the flagship of British industry and a byword for British manufacturing at its best, was failing. In February 1971 Heath felt he had no choice: he intervened and nationalised the company, and 80,000 workers were grateful for the decision. Then, in the latter half of the year, a dispute involving the Upper Clyde Shipbuilders became so politically damaging that the government was forced once more to intervene. The smell of burning rubber on the road as the government performed another rapid U-turn was unmistakeable.

Britain plunges into darkness

In early 1972 it was the miners who entered the national spotlight – a place they would keep in the coming years – and soon the whole country was running short of power. On 9 January the National Union of Miners (NUM) went on strike over pay and the situation was soon so grave that Heath called a state of emergency. The miners organised 'flying pickets' to gather at coal depots, ports and wharves to stop stocks of coal being transported. It was a cold winter, and as coal stocks at power stations dwindled, homes were regularly plunged into darkness and Britain was put on a three-day week. The government urged people to 'Think before you switch on'. Heating was banned in restaurants, cinemas and other public places. Big Ben, Marble Arch and other public monuments were no longer floodlit.

Heath's solution to the crisis was to set up the independent Wilberforce Inquiry to advise on miners' pay. Unfortunately for Heath, the inquiry found in the miners' favour, stating that they should get a pay rise in the region of 20 per cent – the Coal Board's original offer had been 7.5 per cent. The NUM eventually settled for 27 per cent, but by then the strike had changed the political landscape. It was widely perceived that Heath had been cowed and that the police could not control mass pickets. The strike also emboldened the radicals in the unions and in the Labour Party, who had seen what militancy could do.

MINERS AND WIVES UNITED

One of the noticeable things about the miners' strike of 1972 was the degree to which the mining community, the other unions and the public in general were almost universally sympathetic towards it. Unlike the strike of 1984, which divided mining communities, there was a powerful sense of unity. These cheerful miners' wives from Keresley in the West Midlands were on a rally at Tower Hill, London, in 1972. In contrast to this good-natured show of support, in 1984 Keresley folk fell out with the neighbouring miners of Daw Mill, who carried on working; the bad feeling between the communities lasted for years. But back in 1972 the miners were united, and most people felt they deserved the pay rise they were asking for. This attitude would change in 1974, when another miners' strike brought down Heath's government.

By the autumn of 1972, Heath's government was still showing no sign of getting to grips with its various problems. The Prime Minister held cordial meetings with Vic Feather, the General Secretary of the TUC (Trades Union Congress), trying to gain union support for wage control. But union left-wingers Jack Jones and Hugh Scanlon pressed for statutory controls to be imposed on prices, not wages. The talks failed. Heath was forced to introduce statutory controls to counter inflation – knowing that an arm-wrestle with the unions was bound to follow.

A day of national protest

The government's handling of the economy continued to falter. In the budget of March 1973, Chancellor Anthony Barber cut taxation but not public spending; inflationary pressures increased. A month later the unions gave vent to their anger at rising prices and the government's attempt at wage restraints: on 1 May more than 1.5 million workers came out on strike in a 'day of national protest and stoppage'. It was a powerful shot across the bows of Heath's ship of state.

Heath had pinned his hopes on the new Industrial Relations Act, with its putative three-way agreement between the government, the CBI (Confederation of British Industry) and the TUC. But the unions resented the curb on wages and conditions, while the employers resented the squeeze on profits. Without mutual cooperation, the government found out the hard way that their Industrial Relations Act was unworkable and they were unable to enforce it. By the summer of 1973 the government had not so much reined in the unions as retreated before their power. For many in the country – especially Conservative supporters – the Strawbs' got it right with their 1973 chart hit, 'Part of the Union', some of the lyrics of which ran: 'So though I'm a working man/ I can ruin the government's plan/ Though I'm not too hard/ The sight of my card/ Makes me some kind of superman.'

COMMONWEALTH ISSUES

In the early 1970s, many Britons were still nostalgic for the old empire and its reincarnation as the Commonwealth. Sporting fixtures – in particular cricket and rugby – against the likes of Australia, New Zealand, India and the West Indies were often highlights of the year. South Africa, with its apartheid regime, remained excluded from the Commonwealth, although Ted Heath was less severe in his policy towards the country than Wilson had been. But if Britons welcomed Commonwealth sportsmen, their attitude towards immigrants was more ambivalent. Enoch Powell had stirred, or rather inflamed, the debate about immigration with his infamous 'rivers of blood' speech in 1968. In 1971 the Conservative government showed its ongoing concern over the issue with an Act that imposed restrictions on immigrants from Commonwealth countries.

But as a previous Conservative Prime Minister, Harold Macmillan, knew only too well, events could blow political intentions well off course. In 1971

'STRIKE OFF'
Jack Jones, head of the Transport and General Workers' Union, faces the press at Transport House after calling off the dock strike on 16 August, 1972. All 42,000 of Britain's dockers had come out on strike on 28 July in protest against compulsory redundancies. On 4 August the government ordered a state of emergency. Eventually a committee co-chaired by Jones brokered a deal acceptable to the dockers.

Jones himself was considered to be one of the most powerful men in the country during the 1970s. Born in Liverpool, the son of a docker, he was a volunteer in the Spanish Civil War, where in one of those strange coincidences he met the young Edward Heath, who was part of a fact-finding student delegation. Jones was wounded in action and returned to Britain, where he began his career as a trade unionist. He died in 2009 at the age of 96.

General Idi Amin had come to power in Uganda, a signed-up Commonwealth country, through a military coup. In August 1972 he launched an economic war, aimed primarily against the country's Asian population. The Asian community in Uganda had been settled there for about a century and had prospered, leading to feelings of resentment among some of Uganda's majority black population. Idi Amin himself called the Asians 'bloodsuckers', and now he ordered the immediate expulsion of all Asians who were not Ugandan citizens – about 60,000 people, most of whom held British passports.

The move took the Conservative government completely by surprise. Attempts at negotiation achieved nothing and Britain was left with no choice but to accept the arrival of around 30,000 Ugandan-Asians who were forced from their homes with little other than the clothes they stood in, their businesses and wealth having been expropriated by the Ugandan government. Others went to Australia, Canada, India and Pakistan, while some settled in countries outside the Commonwealth. The first arrivals flew into the UK on 18 September, 1972.

Many Britons were far from happy about this sudden influx. Leicester city council took out newspaper advertisements in an attempt to deter the new immigrants from settling there. And Cabinet papers, released after 30 years, showed that the government actually discussed packing them off to a British-owned island. Yet despite fears over the mass arrival, the Asians from Uganda settled well into British society. Back in Uganda, the loss of their business acumen and activity was a disaster for the economy there.

CHILLY WELCOME

The first Asians expelled from Uganda by President Idi Amin began to arrive at Stansted Airport in Essex (right) on 18 September, 1972. The refugees, some of whom had British passports, were moved to military camps, such as RAF Stradishall in Suffolk. They were then allocated accommodation around the country by the Uganda Resettlement Board. Leicester, Bradford and Corby were among the locations favoured by the board.

STICKY WICKET

In March 1970 ground staff at the Oval cricket ground lay new turf behind barbed wire (left) in preparation for the arrival of the South African team in the summer. The barbed wire was to stop anti-apartheid demonstrators wrecking the wicket. South Africa had been expelled from the British Commonwealth in 1961, with the imposition of trade sanctions and exclusion from sporting events. As it turned out, the 1970 cricket tour never took place. On 22 May, after pressure from the government, the Cricket Council withdrew their invitation to the South Africans. Instead, England played a Rest of the World team, which included several South African players alongside the likes of Gary Sobers and Intikhab Alam.

PROTESTING FOR A FAIR, NON-RACIST RHODESIA

Rhodesia would be an ongoing problem for the British government throughout the decade. These demonstrators in Whitehall (above) are protesting against the signing of the Anglo-Rhodesian agreement by Foreign Secretary Sir Alec Douglas-Home in November 1971. Some of the placards accuse him of a sell-out on a par with Neville Chamberlain's agreement with Hitler over Czechoslovakia in 1938. The agreement signed with Ian Smith, prime minister of the all-white government in a

self-declared independent Rhodesia, did hold out the prospect of black majority rule, but in a nebulous and distant future. Too far in the future for the black population of Rhodesia, who rejected the agreement almost unanimously. Black rebels led by Joshua Nkomo and Robert Mugabe launched an armed guerrilla campaign, which became known as the 'Bush War' by the white population of Rhodesia. After seven years of bitter conflict, they brought the Smith government to its knees.

In 1979 Margaret Thatcher, Britain's newly elected Prime Minister, succeeded in getting all parties round a conference table, where it was agreed to hold elections under international supervision the following year. Those elections were won by Mugabe – his ZANU supporters were accused of intimidation but the allegations were ignored. In March 1980 he became the first black prime minister of Rhodesia, now renamed Zimbabwe. Sadly this was far from the end of the country's troubles.

ANTI-MARKETEERS

In October 1971 Parliament voted to join the European Economic Community (EEC), aka the Common Market, but not everyone was happy about it. A diverse group of protesters brought a petition signed by some 750,000 fellow anti-Marketeers to Downing Street on 2 May, 1972 (below). The historian Sir Arthur Bryant is in the centre of the group with unionist Len Murray on the right (both wearing hats), and Labour MP Tony Benn to the left of Bryant. Some feared an erosion of British sovereignty and culture; some pointed to the cost of compensating New Zealand farmers to the tune of £100 million for the loss of their British export market; others were critical of Europe's Common Agricultural Policy (CAP), by which EEC countries had to buy each other's farm produce regardless of whether it could be obtained more cheaply elsewhere.

INTO EUROPE

The prospect of joining the European Economic Community (EEC) provoked very mixed emotions in Britain. Many felt that 'Britishness' was already endangered: closer ties with Europe might extinguish it altogether, just as the introduction of decimal coinage in 1971 consigned the shilling of 12 old pence to history (see pages 38-9). But conversely, just as this antipathy toward Europe was gaining pace, more and more people were visiting the place. Europe was becoming an ever more popular holiday destination. In 1970 around 6 million Britons enjoyed the beauty and beaches of Spain, France and Italy. A year later the figure had increased by another million; by the end of the decade it stood at 10 million. People returned with decidedly un-British notions of cuisine, such as pasta and paella. Pizza restaurants began to spring up at home, and wine started to make inroads into the market for the nation's favourite alcoholic beverage – beer.

continued on page 41

D DAY – BRITAIN GOES DECIMAL

Discussions of metrication had begun in Parliament as far back as the 19th century. At long last, Britain was adopting an important element of the metric system by converting to a decimal currency. The gradual changeover had begun under Labour back in 1968 with the introduction of new 5 pence and 10 pence coins, which were interchangeable with the old shilling and 2 shilling coins. Now, the time for such subtlety was over: the date for the complete changeover to decimal was set for 15 February, 1971.

To prepare the public the government launched a massive publicity campaign. Hoardings like this one (right) went up all over the country to get across the value of the new money relative to the old. Tables were posted up in shops (top left) to inform buyers how much their pounds, shillings and pence would be worth after the change. And school-children (bottom left) were given classes on the new money.

The old units of 12 pence to the shilling and 24 shillings to the pound were replaced by 100 pence to the pound, counted in units of ten. The new money included ½p, 1p, 2p, 5p, 10p and 50 pence coins (the 20p coin was not introduced until 1982). Wherever possible, old coins stayed in use – the sixpence became 2½p, the old shilling became 5p and 2 shillings (2 bob) became 10p. But there was no place for the old 12-sided threepenny bit, which went the way of the crown and half-crown: it ceased to be legal tender in August 1971. Many mourned the passing of the old currency, but most people just got on with it. Millions of coin machines had to be adapted, and some 9,000 taxi cabs had to convert their meters.

Before D Day people worried, and after it many moaned, but in fact the changeover went quite smoothly. Shop assistants who had studied the conversion tables were pleasantly surprised to find that they did not have to convert old values into new – all they had to do was add up in new money. Over time the coinage was modified. In 1982 the 20 pence piece was introduced and smaller, lighter versions of 10 pence and 50 pence pieces were brought in respectively in 1993 and 1998, the year in which the £2 coin also arrived.

HATS OFF TO EUROPE

One of the most eagerly awaited visitors to the Royal Ascot race meeting every year was Gertrude Shilling, whose hats and outfits, created by her son David, both a milliner and sculptor, mixed flamboyance with topicality. This one, paraded in June 1973, was worn to celebrate Britain officially becoming a member of the European Economic Community – along with Eire and Denmark – on 1 January, 1973. The hat displays the names of the nine member countries, while the dress flaunts translations of 'Cheers' in different European languages.

For Ted Heath, Britain's entry into Europe was the realisation of a dream he had worked assiduously to bring about. And he was convinced that the EEC would bring wealth and cultural enrichment to the country. Heath's vision broadly remained that of the Conservatives until the late Eighties, when Margaret Thatcher began increasingly to create a mood of Euroscepticism in the party.

Ted Heath was a proud Europhile and it was arguably his most significant achievement to take Britain – some of it kicking and screaming – into the EEC. He had been involved in previous negotiations for Britain's entry, but back in 1963 and again in 1967 President de Gaulle had famously and unambiguously said 'Non'. Now France had Georges Pompidou at the helm, and he and Heath were on friendly terms; Heath's French accent may have been Dalek-like, but at least he spoke the language with a degree of competence. Back home, he had a hard job to put across the case for Britain's entry. There was a suspicion of European bureaucrats and laws; a fear that the French language would dominate English – Jim Callaghan was to state publicly that 'the language of Chaucer and Shakespeare' would be under threat if Britain joined the EEC; and a concern that a Eurocentric approach would diminish the role of the Commonwealth still further.

Curious alliances

In 1971 Heath and Pompidou held a joint press conference to announce that Britain would be allowed to join the EEC. But entry still depended on a parliamentary vote at Westminster. All over the country debates were held on the merits or otherwise of joining. The issue divided the political parties into pro and anti-Europe factions, with old political enemies suddenly teaming up with each other to do battle. Harold Wilson changed from his previous pro stance to anti, claiming that Heath's terms of entry did not sufficiently benefit Britain. The Labour left – veteran anti-marketeers – were mistrustful of his switch of allegiance, but lined up behind him nonetheless. Pro-European Labour MPs, led by the former Chancellor Roy Jenkins, campaigned with the Tories, led by Heath.

In October 1971 a vote was finally held in Parliament and the pro-Europeans won by a respectable 112 votes; 69 Labour MPs voted with the government. On 1 January, 1973, Britain officially became a member of the EEC, along with the Republic of Ireland and Denmark, bringing the number of member states to nine. With a Union Jack flying from the EEC's headquarters in Brussels and a celebratory torchlit procession in the city's streets, Heath and the pro-Europeans had every reason to celebrate. Over the next few months some 1,000 British civil servants would join their counterparts in Belgium. It was the dawn of a new era, but disagreement over Europe would continue to haunt British politics for decades to come. Within three years Britain would hold a referendum under a Labour government to decide whether the country should remain in the EEC. Heath himself later regarded Britain's entry as his greatest achievement.

'... we will find there is a great cross-fertilisation of knowledge and information, not only in business but in every other sphere. And this will enable us to be more efficient and more competitive in gaining more markets not only in Europe but in the rest of the world.'

Prime Minister Edward Heath, on taking Britain into the EEC

ROCKING THE BOAT
Alongside Ted Heath's rosy view of Britain's
place in the EEC there were several groups
who were less than happy at the prospect.
Fishermen, for example, were angry that
the country was prepared to surrender its
12-mile inshore fishing limit in the interests
of the Common Market. In September 1971
representatives of the protesting fishermen
sailed up the Thames (left) to the House
of Commons before handing in a petition
at 10 Downing Street.

The Cod War and the Cold War

European foreign affairs were far from plain sailing for the government. On 1 September, 1972, Britain fell into a dispute with Iceland about fishing in waters off the Icelandic coast. The Cod War, as it was quickly dubbed, was the second fishing dispute to have erupted between Britain and Iceland. The first was in 1958, and a third would break out in 1975. The term 'war' was perhaps a misnomer, but deliberate collisions and the cutting of fishing nets created tension and animosity between the two countries. Eventually, in 1976, the dispute was ended through the intervention of NATO, to which both countries belonged.

The name Cod War was a tabloid pun on Cold War, a stand-off situation that still formed an icy backdrop to world affairs: the Soviet Union and its Eastern bloc allies were never far from national concerns. By the early 1970s the KGB had reputedly built up a huge number of operatives in London. It was a difficult situation for the Foreign Secretary, Sir Alec Douglas-Home: he could turn a blind eye and hope for the best, or he could attempt to do something about the potential threat. In September 1971 he opted to expel 105 Soviets from Britain – so-called diplomats, journalists and trade representatives. It was, and remains, the largest number of officials expelled by any Western power. Labour accused Douglas-Home of over-reacting, but a later defector, Oleg Gordievsky, claimed that the action had made a significant dent in the Soviet Union's spying operations. In a reprisal, the Soviets sent home 18 officials from the British embassy in Moscow.

SEXUAL POLITICS

At the dawn of the 1970s, despite the rise of the feminist movement in the previous decade, Britain was still a male-dominated society. Not only did men hold all the top jobs, but more often than not men still earned more than women, even when they were employed in the same jobs. But feminists continued to plug away, slowly making inroads into the prevailing consciousness.

An early blow was struck by a young academic named Germaine Greer, who in 1970 published *The Female Eunuch*. The book became seminal, launching a thousand feminist crusades and throwing lifelines to countless women for whom sexual politics was not something to be studied but an oppression to be lifted. Greer, a straight-talking Australian, had won a research scholarship at Cambridge

LIBBERS AND RIBBERS

In a Women's Lib parade in London in March 1971 (right), one woman hoists aloft a cross festooned with symbols of female 'oppression' – a silk stocking, shopping bag, apron and pearls, with rubber gloves slipped onto the ends of the crosspiece. A cornerstone of the women's movement was the magazine *Spare Rib*, co-founded by Marsha Rowe (above, seated) and Rosie Boycott (standing), which encouraged women to break out of the submissive or passive role and become more self-reliant. A regular column explained how to cope with practical problems such as changing a tyre or putting up a shelf, the traditional domain of husbands. In 1973 Boycott, Rowe and Carmen Callil founded Virago, a publishing company dedicated to publishing books written by women.

FEMALE ROLE MODEL
Germaine Greer had arrived in Britain from Australia in 1964 and studied for a doctorate at Newnham College, Cambridge. She taught at Warwick University from 1968 to 1972 when, following the success of *The Female Eunuch*, she began to get more media work. Greer has continued to combine academic teaching with media interests and writing. In 1999 she published *The Whole Woman*, hailed as a sequel to her earlier bestseller, in which she discussed the effects of the health industry on women, including issues such as breast implants and in vitro fertilisation.

in the mid-60s. One contemporary remembered her holding forth at a formal dinner on how women's liberation would never proceed as long as they had to wear cone-like bras that bore no resemblance to the female anatomy. (Ironically, in the next decade, it was precisely the garment that Madonna would choose to assert liberation in a very different way.)

Greer's central thesis was that women were repressed by traditional society, with its nuclear families and conventional suburban attitudes, and consumerism. From an early age, women were taught a particular type of passive femininity and when they grew up, this stereotypical femininity caused them to feel isolated, powerless and sexually unfulfilled. They became, in a word, eunuchs. Greer believed that to liberate themselves women had to revolt, not evolve. As Greer expressed it: 'The revolutionary woman must know her enemies, the doctors, psychiatrists, health visitors, priests, marriage counsellors, policemen, magistrates

and genteel reformers, all the authoritarians and dogmatists who flock about her with warnings and advice.' *The Female Eunuch* first arrived in London in the autumn of 1970. By the following spring it was well on its way towards its position as a feminist classic.

Gay Liberation

Sexuality in the 1970s was more than a feminist issue. Permissiveness – a 'creation' of the Sixties – remained an ideal to fight for, or a curse to be resisted, depending on perspective. And like the women's movement, homosexuals were a group striving for social equality and civil rights. The 1967 Sexual Offences Act had legalised sex in private between consenting men over the age of 21. In October 1970 the UK branch of the Gay Liberation Front held its first meeting at the London School of Economics, which was still a hotbed of radicalism. The GLF were energetic and sometimes militant in promoting gay rights. In 1972 they occupied the offices of the London listings magazine *Time Out* to persuade the magazine to allow gay advertisements in its personal pages.

The GLF's most memorable protest was the disruption in 1971 of a meeting organised by the Festival of Light – an evangelical Christian group that counted Mary Whitehouse and Malcolm Muggeridge among its supporters. The meeting was held at the Methodist Central Hall in London, where it was infiltrated by GLF members. Some, dressed in drag, ostentatiously began to kiss in public. Others blew trumpets and waved banners, while others released mice among the bemused audience. Another group managed to find their way down to the basement where they switched off all the lights.

Wicked wizards of *Oz*

Supporters of the Festival of Light saw themselves as part of the vanguard in the battle to stem the rising tide of sexual permissiveness. Undoubtedly they reflected the views of a great many people, the mythical middle-Englanders for whom tolerance of changing mores had its limits. Sometimes even the state dug in its heels over 'public morals'. One such instance came in 1971 with the notorious prosecution of the editors of *Oz* magazine over their 'School Kids Issue'.

The *Oz* editors had invited 20 teenagers to edit an issue of the underground magazine, and the youngsters duly gave their views on matters ranging from education to sexuality. The issue included a cartoon, drawn by a 15-year-old, of a 'sexualised' Rupert Bear. When the Obscene Publications Squad got wind of this they raided the *Oz* offices, then charged the editors with obscenity and intent to corrupt the young. The trial was a showcase for Censorship versus Permissiveness. Censorship won, until the verdict was overturned on appeal.

Later in the decade, in 1977, Mary Whitehouse privately sued Denis Lemon, editor of *Gay News*, for publishing a poem about a gay Roman centurion's

COMING OUT AS GAY
Gay men and women in the UK struggled for social acceptance in the Seventies, but they did make significant progress. In 1970 the Gay Liberation Front was founded and the following year saw the first gay march, demanding that the legal age of consent for homosexual men be lowered from 21. The publication *Gay News* was founded in 1972; the first gay telephone helpline followed in 1973. In 1976 the singer Tom Robinson wrote the song 'Glad to Be Gay' to mark Gay Pride Week, when gays like this couple (left), picnicking by the Houses of Parliament, came out to declare their sexuality publicly and with pride.

feelings of love for Christ on the cross. Despite heavyweight literary figures such as Bernard Levin and Margaret Drabble appearing to testify that *Gay News* was a responsible newspaper, Lemon lost the case. Whitehouse was delighted: 'I'm rejoicing because I saw the possibility of Our Lord being vilified. Now it's been shown that He won't be.'

But the tide had turned against Mary Whitehouse and like-minded souls. Underpinning the advance of gay and women's rights was the Glam pop culture in which sexual ambiguity – and sometimes overt homosexuality – took on a higher profile. Another sign of changing attitudes came in November 1970, when the *Sun* launched a new feature that managed to offend both Whitehouse and her supporters and the feminists: the daily topless model, or Sun 'stunna', on page 3.

Cosmo Girl

Two new magazines that launched in the UK in 1972 spoke to women in different ways. *Cosmopolitan* was glossy and sassy, devoting column inches not only to fashion tips but to sexual topics such as orgasms and contraception. It appealed to young, upwardly mobile, professional women for whom magazines featuring knitting patterns and recipes no longer cut the mustard. *Spare Rib*, on the other hand, was anti-gloss: a descendant of the 1960s underground press, it was an issues-led magazine tying feminist ideals to a socialist agenda. It tried to change attitudes, not least those of women themselves. Its radical timbre riled many, and W H Smith at first refused to stock it. Nevertheless, *Spare Rib* soon reached a steady circulation of about 20,000 copies per month.

SCHOOL'S OUT
In October 1970 the editors of the underground magazine *Oz* drew attention to the preliminary hearing for their court case by dressing up as schoolboys. Accused of obscenity, Richard Neville (left), James Anderson (centre) and Felix Dennis (right) had the support of various celebrities, including John Lennon and Yoko Ono. They were defended by John Mortimer and Geoffrey Robertson – eminent lawyers known for their work in aid of liberal and controversial causes – but nonetheless the three were found guilty. They were saved from jail by a successful appeal.

Although gender equality was very much on the agenda, real advances for women in the workplace were slow in coming. But the decade did have some milestones. On 26 March, 1973, the Stock Exchange, a 200-year-old male bastion, admitted women for the first time. The following year, BBC2 featured the first female national newsreader in Angela Rippon. In 1978 ITN launched their answer to Rippon in the form of Anna Ford. In 1975 the Sex Discrimination Act formally addressed issues of equality in the workplace.

The greatest feminist milestone was achieved not by the radical left but by the Conservative Party. In 1976 Margaret Thatcher became the first woman to lead a political party in Britain, then in 1979 she became the first – and so far only – woman Prime Minister, achievements that must have seemed unthinkable in the Sixties. Looking back on the early years of *Spare Rib*, Rosie Boycott stated: 'The newly emerging feminist movement wanted to get women out of the typing pools and away from the kitchen sinks and into the boardrooms of the land.' Slowly but surely, it was making progress towards that aim, and Thatcher's success boosted that progress – a fact appreciated by women even in the Labour Party.

MISS PROTEST

Women's libbers outside the Royal Albert Hall in November 1971 (below), protesting against the Miss World contest being held inside. The annual beauty parade became a high-profile target for feminists, who accused it of trivialising and demeaning women, judging them by their bodies, not their brains or achievements. The previous year demonstrators had thrown flour bombs during the contest, while in 1969 they waved placards with slogans such as 'Mis-fortune demands equal pay for women' and 'Mis-conception demands free abortion for all women'. If the contest attracted feminist ire, it was also a curious barometer of public morality: in 1974 the Miss World crown was won by a young Welsh woman named Helen Morgan, representing the UK, but she was pressurised into resigning after just four days when it was revealed that she was a single mother.

MAKING NEWS

Angela Rippon (above) became television's first female national newsreader in 1974 and did much to project the feminist ideal of a woman valued for her professional expertise. Born in Plymouth, the daughter of a Royal Marine, Rippon grew up in Devon and left school at 17. She worked in BBC local radio before beginning her career as a newsreader on BBC2. Rippon oozed dignity and calm and soon became a national celebrity. She presented other shows, including the 1977 Eurovision Song Contest, which was held in London after the UK's victory the previous year with Brotherhood of Man and 'Save Your Kisses for Me'. In the same year she co-presented the BBC's motoring show, *Top Gear*, in its first incarnation. But her most celebrated performance came at Christmas 1976 with the nation's most popular comedy duo, Morecambe and Wise. Rippon emerged from behind a spoof news desk to reveal a long and shapely pair of legs, then proceeded to 'face the music and dance'.

TROUBLES AND STRIFE

BOVVER BOYS
Looking more like a clown than a hooligan, a 'fan' is ejected from Highbury Stadium, home of Arsenal, during a match against Manchester United on 25 August, 1973 (above). The relaxed crowd, soaking up the warm weather, seem amused by the diversion. More menacing elements in football crowds were the skinhead gangs, who often went to matches looking for a fight. They cut their hair ultrashort – hence the name 'skinhead' – and wore Doc Martens boots, like these ones being aggressively displayed on a pub table in 1978 (left).

If the late Sixties youth culture could be crudely characterised by a mood of love and peace, the 1970s saw a more ugly, more violent strain emerging in society, perhaps symbolised by two notoriously violent cult films, *Straw Dogs* (1971) and *A Clockwork Orange* (1972). Not that this happened straightaway. The early Seventies still had the fading incense of hippy ideals. Yet, bit by bit, the Seventies

came to be the decade when anger, often born of political frustration or despair, replaced optimistic protest. With youth culture, this anger was to explode in the Punk movement, which in the middle of the decade broke out like adolescent acne on the face of society.

On the terraces

Of course, anger and violence were not an invention of the Seventies. Football hooligans fighting on the terraces or outside football grounds had become familiar news stories by the late Sixties. But hooligans in the early part of the decade – usually skinhead gangs sporting braces and Doc Martens 'bovver boots' – lacked the sinister sophistication of the violent gangs that became notorious in the mid to latter years of the Seventies and in the early Eighties. By then these gangs, or 'firms', had names such as the Gooners (Arsenal), the Inter-City Firm (West Ham), Headhunters (Chelsea) and Red Army (Manchester United), and their violence was more orchestrated.

A turning point in the public perception of football hooliganism was the stabbing to death of a Blackpool fan during a match against Bolton Wanderers in August 1974. It was believed to be the first death caused by hooliganism at an English football ground. Football-related violence continued to be a running sore throughout the rest of the decade. It would reach a nadir in the 1980s, with the banning of English clubs from European competition because of persistent trouble-making by their fans attending games in Europe.

The Angry Brigade

A more explosive – literally – expression of radical anger came through the activities of the enigmatic Angry Brigade. At a time when Germany had the Baader-Meinhof gang and Italy the Red Brigades, a militant anarchist group calling themselves the Angry Brigade emerged in Britain. They were young men and women with radical left ideals and militancy to match, who believed that violence rather than words was the way to bring about the change they wished to see in bourgeois, capitalist Western society. Although never as ruthlessly violent as their European counterparts, the Angry Brigade were extremely active. Between 1970 and 1972 they planted, it is thought, more than 20 bombs. Their targets included banks, government offices, embassies and the homes of establishment figures.

Perhaps the most symbolically dramatic action of the Angry Brigade was their attack on the Biba department store, an icon of Sixties fashion and hippy chic. On 1 May, 1971, as hundreds of shoppers were evacuated, a blast erupted from one of the storerooms. No-one was hurt. The Brigade left an explanatory communiqué, part of which read 'The only thing you can do with modern slavehouses – called boutiques – is WRECK THEM'. The message also adapted a line from a Bob Dylan song, 'It's Alright Ma (I'm Only Bleeding)' – instead of Dylan's 'dying', the line went 'If you're not busy being born, you're busy buying'. It was a watershed moment: the message could have been pure Sixties, but the action that went with it came to be seen as pure Seventies.

In August that same year, police arrested members of the Angry Brigade in north London. Their trial at the Old Bailey began in May 1972 and lasted until 6 December, one of the longest criminal trials in British history. Four members of the brigade – three men and one woman – were each sentenced to ten years in prison for 'conspiracy to cause explosions'.

The Troubles

The Angry Brigade's antics seemed like an Aunt Sally at a vicarage fete compared with the violence in Northern Ireland – violence that spread to the British mainland. In August 1969, the 'battle of Bogside' in Londonderry and rioting in Belfast had compelled the government in Northern Ireland to take the momentous step of calling in British troops to ease the pressure on the Royal Ulster Constabulary (RUC). The military presence would remain for four decades.

The Stormont government tried to put together a programme of reform to ease tensions, but they were not quick or radical enough. Sectarian battle lines between Protestant Unionists and Catholic Nationalists, or Republicans, were crystalising. By the end of December 1969, the IRA had split into two factions: the Official IRA and the Provisional IRA, a group prepared to use violent force to gain their objectives. Nationalist militancy was matched by loyalist entrenchment. The paramilitary Ulster Volunteer Force, formed in 1966, was bolstered in 1971 by the UDA, the Ulster Defence Association. Soon sectarian murders all over the province became regular depressing news items, with the British Army caught in the middle. In March 1971, the Northern Ireland prime minister, Major James Chichester-Clarke, resigned and was replaced by Brian Faulkner.

MAYHEM IN ULSTER
The Troubles in Northern Ireland intensified in 1972, especially after Bloody Sunday, when members of the Parachute Regiment shot dead 13 unarmed Catholics on a demonstration in Derry on 30 January. The bitterness between loyalist and republican communities was seen daily in murders, maimings and bombings. Children were often in the front line, like these boys (right), hijacking a car after the killing of a British soldier by an IRA gunman in West Belfast on 12 April, 1972. One of the most notorious loyalist enclaves was the Shankill Road area, shown here (above) in June 1972 with the menacing figures of UDA members manning the barricades outside The Standard Bar. The Shankill and neighbouring republican Falls Road saw much of the sectarian violence in Belfast.

From internment to Sunningdale

Faulkner tried to cut the ground from beneath the IRA by inviting the Social Democratic and Labour Party (SDLP) – nationalists committed to constitutional politics – to participate more fully in the Stormont government. But the violence had gone too far and the SDLP abandoned Stormont. As bloodshed on the streets continued, on 9 August, 1971, with the agreement of Ted Heath, Faulkner imposed internment – indefinite detention without trial – of IRA suspects. In a series of dawn raids, police and soldiers detained some 350 individuals. Violent protests ensued and more than 20 people lost their lives in three days. The protests went on throughout the year, including strikes and the refusal to pay council rents.

On Sunday 30 January, 1972, a Catholic Civil Rights march took place in Derry, in defiance of a ban on parades and marches. Members of the British Parachute Regiment took up position in the city centre in case of trouble. When missiles were hurled, they responded with live bullets – they would claim later they had been fired on. Thirteen unarmed civilians fell dead and the history of Ireland was scarred with another 'Bloody Sunday'. The killings galvanised support for the IRA and set off a surge of anger in the Republic. The British government tried to get a grip on the deteriorating situation by suspending the government in Stormont to rule the province directly from Westminster. But in all it was a grim year for Northern Ireland, with more than 300 civilians killed and almost 5,000 injured.

BLOODY SUNDAY

On Sunday 30 January, 1972, British troops line Irish Catholics up against a wall to be searched (above). Seamus Heaney wrote his poem 'Casualty' on the events of that terrible day:

> 'After they shot dead
> The thirteen men in Derry.
> **PARAS THIRTEEN**, the walls said
> **BOGSIDE NIL.'**

Immediately after the killings, up to 30,000 outraged protesters in the Irish Republic besieged the British Embassy in Dublin; on 2 February it was burned down. In April 1972 a government inquiry exonerated the soldiers on duty, but accusations of a cover up would not go away. The calls for a public inquiry finally bore fruit in 1998, when Prime Minister Tony Blair commissioned Lord Saville to conduct an investigation. His report, published in June 2010, found that the people who died that day were innocent victims, 'none of whom was posing a threat of causing death or injury'.

WINDOW WITNESS
One of the leading activists on the Republican side in Northern Ireland was Bernadette Devlin, who was elected MP for Mid Ulster at the age of just 21, the youngest woman to enter Parliament. Here, a week after Bloody Sunday, she watches as thousands of Catholics march in protest. When Home Secretary Reginald Maudling stated in the House of Commons that the soldiers were firing in self-defence, Devlin was so infuriated that she punched him, an action that got her temporarily suspended from Parliament.

In the summer of 1973, Heath's government attempted to re-establish political power in Northern Ireland by setting up an assembly that would elect an executive made up of both Unionists and Nationalists. There were plans for a Council of Ireland, which would concern itself with matters of mutual concern for the North and the Republic, such as tourism and conservation. The fragile assembly came into being in June, including a majority in favour of power sharing and a sizable minority who opposed it. Nevertheless, political progress had been achieved. By November 1973 an executive had been agreed on, with Brian Faulkner as chief executive and the SDLP leader Gerry Fitt as deputy chief executive.

The next significant political building-block came in December 1973 with the Sunningdale Agreement, named after the Berkshire town where the negotiators met. There, Edward Heath, the Irish Taoiseach (prime minister) Liam Cosgrave and the leaders of the pro-agreement parties of Northern Ireland drew up plans for the Council of Ireland. The council's executive power was limited, but not limited enough for many Unionists, who saw it as the tip of an emerald-green iceberg. In the British general election of February 1974, anti-agreement Unionists registered their protest at the ballot box. Of a possible 12 parliamentary seats, their candidates won 11. The new assembly was not quite yet dead in the water – on 14 May, 1974, it reaffirmed its support for the Sunningdale Agreement – but it was only a matter of time before it would collapse under the forces of division.

WHO RUNS THE COUNTRY?

By the autumn of 1973, problems were piling up for Edward Heath and his premiership was looking increasingly shaky. Efforts to address the economy had largely failed, not helped by the weakness of sterling over the summer. His Cabinet were generally perceived to lack dynamism and leadership qualities – especially in contrast with the forceful, straight-talking, often charismatic leaders of the unions. Scandal had forced the resignation of high-profile Tories from both the government and House of Lords. But Heath's biggest problem was oil, which in less than two years had risen in price more than five-fold, driving up inflation.

HEAVYWEIGHT MP Cyril Smith, the jovial Liberal MP for Rochdale, weighed over 29 stone at his peak. Here he is during the February 1974 election campaign, being hoisted aloft by a forklift truck.

UNION MUSCLE

'For years afterwards, it was a decade that could scarcely be mentioned without … conjuring up images of … power cuts, the three-day week … and all-powerful trade unions.'

Alwyn W Turner, from *Crisis What Crisis?: Britain in the 1970s*

OIL CRISIS

In 1972 a barrel of oil cost under $2; by early 1974 the price had risen to more than $11. The rise was the result of an oil embargo by OPEC (the Oil Producing and Exporting Countries) following the Israeli victory over Arab states in the Yom Kippur War in October 1973. The huge hike in the crude oil price led to a similar hike in petrol and concern about supplies. Long queues formed at service stations (below) as people tried to beat the next price rise and ensure they had some petrol in the tank. The Trade and Industry Secretary Peter Walker appealed to motorists to cut down on petrol consumption and use public transport. Petrol rationing was not introduced, but 18 million ration books were printed and distributed to post offices in case they were needed. They were destroyed only in the summer of 1975 after the threat of rationing had passed. A beneficiary of the petrol crisis was the National Union of Miners, led by Joe Gormley (right). In December 1974 Gormley stated that the days of cheap oil were over and the government would have to turn increasingly to 'indigenous energy sources' – that is to say, to coal.

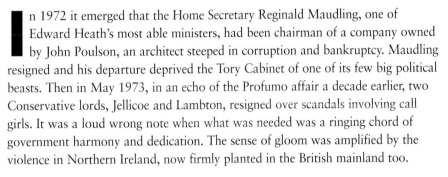

I n 1972 it emerged that the Home Secretary Reginald Maudling, one of Edward Heath's most able ministers, had been chairman of a company owned by John Poulson, an architect steeped in corruption and bankruptcy. Maudling resigned and his departure deprived the Tory Cabinet of one of its few big political beasts. Then in May 1973, in an echo of the Profumo affair a decade earlier, two Conservative lords, Jellicoe and Lambton, resigned over scandals involving call girls. It was a loud wrong note when what was needed was a ringing chord of government harmony and dedication. The sense of gloom was amplified by the violence in Northern Ireland, now firmly planted in the British mainland too.

The price of oil and coal

If matters were not bad enough, events far beyond Heath's control now propelled him into the deepest crisis of his premiership. On 6 October, the Jewish Day of Atonement or Yom Kippur, Arab forces attacked Israel starting the Yom Kippur War. The Israelis were heavily outnumbered, but better equipped. After initial loss of ground, they rapidly gained the upper hand. A ceasefire came into operation on 26 October and both sides stepped back to lick their wounds. The fall-out included a Saudi-led OPEC oil embargo of countries sympathetic to Israel. The price of oil rocketed, quadrupling by the end of the year and feeding a spiral of inflation in the West. In Britain prices in the shops suddenly shot up 10 per cent.

Union opposition to Ted Heath's wages policy now took on a much greater import. When the miners began a ban on overtime on 12 November, 1973, in support of a large wage claim, the government declared a state of emergency the following day. It was the dark days of 1972 all over again, except this time the outcome would be politically fatal for Heath. On 28 November he held talks with the miners' leaders, to no avail. The pitmen were in bullish mood – their leader Joe Gormley remarked to Heath that 'the lads' chests were a mile wide and they thought they were the kings of the castle'.

On 2 December, with chaos looming, Heath resorted to reshuffling his Cabinet, but it was a case of rearranging the deck-chairs on the *Titanic*. His most imaginative move was making the genial Willie Whitelaw the new Employment Secretary. Whitelaw was fresh from negotiating with hardliners in Northern Ireland, and if anyone could sweet-talk the miners, he was the man. Meanwhile, people braced themselves for energy cuts. From 5 December lighting was restricted in streets, offices and shops. Midweek floodlit soccer matches gave way to daylight Sunday afternoon games. A national speed limit of 50mph was imposed on roads

WORKING IN THE DARK
The winter of 1973–4 will be remembered as a time of power cuts and the three-day week. Even when there was power, in some offices heaters and kettles were banned to conserve energy. In the Bond Street office of the quilt manufacturers Slumberdown (above) staff kept warm by wrapping themselves up in their company's products while continuing to work by candlelight. In a DIY shop (above right) the employees donned miners' lamps to enable them to see what they were doing. In general, people all over the country rose to the challenge and carried on – the 'spirit of the Blitz' was often mentioned in newspapers. Old oil lamps, retrieved from attics, and gas lamps used in camping were put to new service. It was reported that one golf driving range was kept open in the evening by illumination from car headlights.

to save petrol. Then, on 13 December, Heath announced that from the end of the month there would be a three-day week, with only newspapers, restaurants, food shops and essential services exempt.

Heath did not give up hope of reaching a settlement with the miners. On 27 December the National Coal Board met the NUM, but again no progress was made. So the new year, 1974, started gloomily. As the three-day week kicked in, Britain once more became a fairyland of candlelit interiors. People became used to television going off air at 10.30pm – but not perhaps to sharing baths and brushing their teeth in the dark, as the government recommended.

Len Murray, now general secretary at the TUC, tried to resolve the deadlock by arguing that the miners were a special case: meeting their demands need not create a precedent for others. But Chancellor Anthony Barber reaffirmed that the government was not for turning. Although Willie Whitelaw still met with NUM officials, his diplomacy yielded nothing. Negotiations and political manoeuvring continued throughout January. Meanwhile, an extra 1.5 million people joined the unemployed register as a result of the three-day week.

The miners upped the ante on 23 January by calling for a ballot on strike action. In a television appearance on 27 January, Heath ratcheted up the tension still further by berating Mick McGahey, the communist Scottish miners' leader, and denouncing the 'brute force of industrial power'. The situation was delicately poised. For the moment, the three-day week was holding up and coal supplies, supplemented by expensive oil imports, were being eked out. Could the government survive until spring, when improved weather would help its cause? Then, on 4 February, the results of the miners' ballot came through: more than 80 per cent had voted for an all-out strike, to begin on 9 February.

CALLS FOR UNITY
Harold Wilson, seen here (left) addressing a press conference in front of a poster proclaiming Labour's election theme, conducted a somewhat lacklustre campaign in February 1974 and many believed he lacked the energy and will to win. His party's manifesto claimed that the Tory government had called the election in panic. It promised to work towards social equality and the elimination of poverty to bring about 'a fundamental ... shift in the balance of power and wealth in favour of working people and their families'.

The Tories distributed posters focusing on the need for a fair pay-and-prices policy (below). Like Labour, they also stressed the need for unity, declaring in their manifesto that to survive the 'grave perils', a 'united people' and a 'strong government' were needed. It was Labour who got the chance to put their brand of unity into action.

To the polls

Heath had been wary of holding an election, believing it would focus too narrowly on the miners' dispute. But now he felt he had no option. On 7 February, two days before the strike, he announced a general election to be held on 28 February. In a televised speech, he made a direct appeal to the nation: 'This time the strife has got to stop. Only you can stop it. It is time for you to speak, with your vote.'

Heath's campaign was on the issue of 'who governs Britain?'. For him, it was high noon between the government and the unions, and he was asking the British people to pull the trigger. Most polls suggested that he would win. But one major stumbling block was news of a trade deficit of £383 million, the highest figure recorded at that time. Another problem was Enoch Powell. Long out of favour with the Tory leadership, Powell had decided to withdraw from the election, but he did not leave it there. Ever the maverick, he was supporting Labour because of their commitment to hold a referendum on Britain's membership of the EEC.

CLIFF-HANGER ELECTION
The rosetted Tory MP Laurance Reed listens
on the doorstep in a typical working-class
street in Bolton in February 1974. The
campaign officially began on 7 February,
and the government gave itself a boost by
lifting the 10.30pm television curfew. Tory
candidates were briefed to make the issue
of who governed Britain – the unions or the
government – the main focus of their
campaign. The Oxford-educated Reed was
the sitting MP for Bolton East, having been
elected in 1970. But he failed to retain his
seat in Heath's showdown election, losing
out to Labour's David Young.

On the eve of the election, Heath gave a
pre-recorded party election broadcast on
television. Here he is in his constituency
headquarters in Sidcup – in the company of
party workers Roger Mountford (left) and
Richard Simmonds – watching himself in
that broadcast. He had told the nation that
it was 'time for your voice to be heard – the
voice of the moderate and reasonable
people of Britain'. He was optimistic of
holding on to power – the election-day issue
of the *Daily Mail* predicted a clear-cut Tory
victory. But unfortunately for Heath the
voice of the people was not enough. He
won marginally more votes than Harold
Wilson, but Britain's first-past-the-post
system gave more seats to Labour.

At one public meeting, Powell was called a 'Judas' by a disenchanted Tory voter.
Powell calmly retorted that Judas was paid, while in contrast he was making a
sacrifice. Harold Wilson, meanwhile, emphasised that he was the man who could
come to a proper working partnership with the unions. The official vehicle for this
was Labour's Social Contract, a joint agreement between Labour and the unions.
It promised to impose price controls and to scrap the Tories' union legislation in
return for union assurances of voluntary wage restraint.

On polling day, more people turned out to vote than ever before – 78.8 per
cent of the electorate. Wilson won by a whisker. In a reverse of the Tory victory
that ousted Attlee in 1951, Labour won fewer votes than the Conservatives but
gained more seats – 301 to 297. The Liberals under Jeremy Thorpe took 14 seats.
Heath discussed with Thorpe the possibility of a coalition government, but it was
clutching at straws. On 4 March, Heath drove to Buckingham Palace and handed
in his resignation to the Queen. Harold Wilson had won his third election and was
about to start his second stint as Prime Minister of a minority government.

A TOUCH OF SPARKLE

During the dark days of power cuts and three-day weeks, there was one aspect of life in Britain that could be counted on to provide some colour – Glam Rock. This distinct and mainly British music phenomenon furnished the nation's youth with a new sound and came with a dramatic, glittering, androgynous look – a curious mix of sci-fi and high camp. It was essentially escapist: the glitter, make-up, jump suits and dyed hair could turn a spotty adolescent into a hero. The fairy godfather of Glam was probably Marc Bolan of T. Rex, and he was soon followed by the likes of Slade, Gary Glitter, Roxy Music, Queen and especially David Bowie.

Glam's appeal went beyond its insistent four-beat rock rhythms, singalong lyrics and throbbing guitar riffs. With the split-up of the Beatles, the death of Jimi Hendrix and the hippy world of folk-ballads and political protest songs fading into memory, Glam felt like a new beginning. It absorbed the prevailing zeitgeist, chiming, for example, with the fresh interest in space – Neil Armstrong had taken his historic walk on the Moon on 21 July, 1969. Silver suits were flaunted by Glam bands, and songs such as Elton John's 'Rocket Man' and David Bowie's 'Life on Mars' took listeners on wistful voyages to distant realms. In days of relentless industrial disputes and a failing economy, Glam – unashamedly superficial, tinselly and fun – was the perfect vehicle for make-believe.

FAIRY GODFATHER OF GLAM
Marc Bolan (right) and T. Rex were the pioneers of Glam rock, blazing a trail that others would follow. Changing style from an acoustic-based folk group, Tyrannosaurus Rex, T. Rex emerged as a hard-hitting electric outfit, scoring a massive hit with 'Hot Love' in 1971, quickly followed by 'Get It On'. The following year, the success continued with 'Telegram Sam' and 'Metal Guru' (both reaching number one), then 'Children of the Revolution' and 'Solid Gold Easy Action'. Bolan strutted his stuff at two enormous sell-out gigs at the Wembley Empire Pool (later the Wembley Arena), but by the end of 1972 Bolan's star had already started to wane. He died in a car crash on Barnes Common in southwest London in 1977, but his music has stood the test of time.

DANCE MOVES
A television treat of the Seventies, particularly for male viewers, was the weekly appearance on *Top of the Pops* of the all-girl dance troupe Pan's People (left). Choreographed by Flick Colby, the six girls would interpret one of the show's featured songs, wearing dance costumes that often exposed generous amounts of flesh. The Pan's People routines lasted until April 1976, when they bowed out to 'Silver Star' by the Four Seasons. They were replaced initially by a troupe called Ruby Flipper, co-managed by Colby, and then later by Legs & Co, who saw out the rest of the decade, lasting on the show until 1981.

ZIGGY STARDUST

David Bowie (left) personified Glam rock like nobody else. He was born David Jones but changed his name in the mid-60s to avoid being confused with Davy Jones of the Monkees. Bowie was the master of theatrical timing: he started his shows with 'Ode to Joy' from Beethoven's ninth symphony, as strobes and dry ice built up the drama. Then the waif-like Bowie would make his entrance on stage, his face white and cheeks rouged, flame-orange hair cresting up in a bouffant and flowing down his neck as a mane. Whatever Bowie wore on stage – like this jumpsuit for a concert in Newcastle – it was talked about afterwards and reported by a gleeful press. At other times he wore denim jeans, an open bomber jacket and silver boxer's boots. Sometimes the costumes were Japanese, sometimes teasingly effeminate – in 1972, in an interview for *Melody Maker*, he announced that he was gay, though later he changed this to bisexual when it was pointed out that he had a wife and child.

On a more serious level, glam-rockers like Bowie and Bolan were challenging some prevailing social prejudices. Homosexuality may have been legalised in 1967, but that did not make it acceptable in the opinions of many. By the way they dressed and acted, glam-rockers made it okay for men to express a feminine side – and made life a little easier for many who came after them.

T-Rextasy and Bowie

With his bouncy corkscrew locks, impish smile and glitter-sprinkled cheeks, Marc Bolan was the first public face of Glam rock. His 1970 single 'Ride a White Swan' brought him and his band T. Rex into the Top Ten charts for the first time; their first mega-hit was 'Hot Love', which reached number one in March 1971. Almost overnight Bolan became a sensation and a leader of fashion. Lurex jackets, tight satin trousers and shaggy hair with an optional hat perched on top (like Bolan's trademark 'topper') became the latest thing.

By 1973 Glam's baton had been passed to David Bowie, a huge fan of the T. Rex front man. Perhaps more than anyone, Bowie personified the spirit of Glam. He first hit the national consciousness in 1969, with his wistful and very topical hit, 'Space Oddity'. It was another three years before he released *The Rise And Fall Of Ziggy Stardust And The Spiders From Mars*, the album that made him a megastar. The record's concept – concept albums were very much the thing in early seventies music – centred on a rock idol named Ziggy performing during the last years of planet Earth. Bowie put on spectacular shows, emerging as Ziggy from clouds of dry ice and rainbows of coloured lights, dressed in costumes that ranged from spangled jump suits to kimonos.

Unlike Bolan, Bowie took the USA by storm. In autumn 1972 Ziggymania criss-crossed the USA, and the furore followed him to Japan in the spring of 1973.

THE SERIOUS SIDE OF GLAM
Fronted by the smooth Bryan Ferry, who conjured up a sleazy retro world of glitzy fashion and 1950s movies, Roxy Music brought a unique art-house style to Glam rock. The band produced a string of hit albums – *For Your Pleasure* (April 1973), *Stranded* (December 1973), *Country Life* (1974). The photograph below shows their classic line-up, standing from left to right: Phil Manzanera (lead guitar); Bryan Ferry (vocals and keyboards); Brian Eno (synthesizer); Rik Kenton (bass guitar); and sitting in front Andy Mackay (saxophone) and Paul Thompson (drums).

Then, on 3 July, 1973, from the stage of the Hammersmith Odeon in London, Bowie stunned his fans by announcing that he was killing Ziggy off: 'This show will stay the longest in our memories, not just because it is the end of the tour but because it is the last show we'll ever do.' It was the high watermark of Glam rock. Bowie would go on to re-invent himself musically, but for many, Ziggy remains his finest hour. As one fan put it, seeing his show was 'like walking into the future'.

Glam variety

There were other, disparate bands who had huge success under the Glam umbrella. Slade, for example, led by Noddy Holder with his trade-mark mutton chops and top hat. The band thrashed out foot-stomping numbers with Holder's intense, frazzled vocals carrying the chorus line to peaks of catchiness: once heard, a Slade song was rarely forgotten. Perhaps their most-enduring hit, a staple of supermarket Christmas muzak even to this day, is the classic 'Merry Christmas Everybody', which first lit up the festive season in 1973.

In complete contrast to foot-stompers like Slade and Gary Glitter, Roxy Music were more atune with Bowie's arthouse odyssey. The silver lamé suits, padded shoulders and platform shoes rooted them firmly in the world of Glam when they first hit the charts with 'Virginia Plain' in 1972. The distinctive vibrato voice of Brian Ferry, their elegant lead singer, with Brian Eno's avant-garde synthesizer gave Roxy a highly original sound. Their 1973 single 'Pyjamarama' added to their reputation, but from then on the band had to adjust to the departure of Eno and Ferry's increasing tendency to nurture a solo crooner career.

YOU SEXY THING
Two of the most consistently successful Seventies acts spanning the divisions of disco, glam and rock were Hot Chocolate (above) and Elton John (right). Fronted by Errol Brown (centre), Hot Chocolate held the distinction of having a chart hit in every year of the Seventies. Their most memorable song was probably 'You Sexy Thing', which reached number two in November 1975, but 'Brother Louie' and 'So You Win Again' were other favourites.

Reginald Kenneth Dwight, better known as Elton John, had a first top ten hit in 1970 with 'Your Song', but it was his 1972 ballad 'Rocket Man', which reached number two, that propelled him to stardom. Working with lyricist Bernie Taupin, Elton combined sweet melodies and sensitive orchestral arrangements with occasional raunchy rock-and-roll. His 1973 album *Goodbye Yellow Brick Road*, which included 'Candle in the Wind' and 'Bennie and the Jets', reached number one in both the UK and the USA, consolidating a career that would last through the decades to come.

TARTAN ARMY

One of the most successful bands of the mid-seventies were the Bay City Rollers, fronted by vocalist Les McKeown, who emerged from Edinburgh to inspire a nationwide craze for tartan among their predominantly girl fans (right). In 1974 they had four hits – 'Remember', 'Shang-a-Lang', 'Summerlove Sensation', and 'All of Me Loves All of You' – then 'Rollermania', as the tabloids called it, swept Britain when they toured the country in 1975. They fronted a kids' TV programme, *Shang-a-Lang*, and had another massive hit with 'Bye, Bye, Baby', but in 1976 cracks began to appear. With the advent of Punk, the Rollers simply faded away.

A couple of years before BCR, another new pop sensation had flown in from the USA, bewitching young girls who wore badges and rosettes declaring their love for the Osmonds (below). Brothers from a Mormon family, the Osmonds had a clean-cut image and songs to match. In 1972 the two youngest, Donny (14) and Jimmy (12), had smash solo hits with 'Puppy Love' and 'Long Haired Lover from Liverpool'.

Heels, hot-pants and loons

Glam rock had its own distinctive fashion that drew on, and in turn influenced, 1970s fashion in general. The most obvious crossover between Glam and non-Glam fashion was the platform shoe. Extreme examples of this chunky style footwear had soles and heels measuring upward of 2 and 5 inches (5 and 10cm) respectively. For the vertically challenged they were the answer to a prayer: worn with a pair of flared loon trousers, they gave everyone the long legs of fashion models. Platforms were worn to work as well as on the dance floor, and men wore them as well as women.

FOLLOWERS OF FASHION

The Seventies may have been the decade that style forgot, but at least the clothes were fun. And there were advantages – platform shoes were a godsend for short people, for example. Among the not-so-tall Glam-rockers who took advantage of them to boost their stage presence were Dave Hill of Slade and Elton John, both of whom pushed heel height to extraordinary proportions. Dungarees came out of the workplace to become an unlikely fashion item. Polka dots, stripes and checks on T-shirts, blouses and even shoes were popular. By the mid-Seventies women were matching textured and coloured tights with blue suede sandals on rope wedges (Russell & Bromley £16.99) or white leather platform shoes (Saxone £8.99).

> ## 'If Britain was so sickly in the seventies, where did people get the money at the time to buy so many records and bold pairs of trousers?'
>
> Andy Beckett, from *When the Lights Went Out: Britain in the Seventies*

For women, 1971 saw the entry of hot pants – tiny, figure-hugging shorts that exposed the thigh, often worn with knee-length boots or high heels. Hot pants could be slinky and satin for the evening, or workaday and denim, and they were even worn in fashionable society. Royal Ascot actually amended its dress code to allow the wearing of hot pants, but stipulated that women had to ensure the 'general effect' of their dress was 'satisfactory'. Hot pants were, in a way, the Seventies' answer to the Sixties' mini skirt, but they had to compete with other 1970s favourites, such as the midi and maxi skirt. As far as hemlines were concerned, this was pretty much a decade of anything goes.

A staple unisex item were loons – low-slung hipster trousers that hugged the backside and thighs before flaring out dramatically from the knee. Naturally, they came in all colours, even tartan, and all sorts of fabrics, from brushed denim to crushed velvet. Although suited to the slinky figure, men and women of all shapes and sizes wore them. On top the perfect match was, for women, a scoop-neck T-shirt with flared draw-string sleeves, for men, perhaps a cheesecloth shirt, with enough top buttons undone to reveal a hairy chest or a pendant – a shark's tooth if you were cool, a medallion if you weren't. Men completed their sexual attraction kit by growing their hair long, cultivating sideburns and splashing on aftershave. Old Spice was popular, as was the rather less sophisticated Brut – as advertised by Henry Cooper and Kevin Keegan – and the teenagers' delight, Hai Karate. For women Revlon launched Charlie in 1975, targeting the young professional generation of *Cosmopolitan* readers.

DRESS STATEMENT

There was something to suit all shapes, sizes and levels of sophistication in Seventies clothes, and what people wore said something about who they were. At the sassy end of the spectrum, fashion outlets such as Mr Freedom boutique, which operated in the King's Road, Chelsea, then in Kensington, sold chic little numbers like the halter-neck spotted sundress or the short striped version with bolero modelled here (above left). For some teenage girls – like these two at Holland Park School, the flagship London comprehensive where Tony Benn sent his children – the hippy look of Afghan coats, jeans and clogs or sneakers was just the thing. Skinheads (above) wore no-nonsense clothes that emphasised their working-class ethos and above all did not look 'hippy'. Sheepskin coats, Doc Marten boots, jeans or Levi Sta-Prest – worn with braces and stopping short above the ankle – were all popular, as were pork-pie and trilby hats.

HAROLD WILSON'S SWANSONG

LABOUR LEFT AND RIGHT
The Labour Party returned to power in March 1974 with a Cabinet packed with seasoned campaigners. On the left of the party were figures such as Michael Foot (below), the new Employment Secretary, whose passion and rhetoric were guaranteed to rally the faithful at party conferences. The right of the party also included political heavyweights, such as the new Chancellor, Denis Healey (bottom), shown brandishing the famous budget box outside Number 11 on 12 November, 1974.

In March 1974 Harold Wilson began his third term as Prime Minister. Unlike Heath's Cabinet, Wilson's oozed experience and talent. Denis Healey – whose red-cheeked visage, bushy eyebrows and mordant wit would become familiar during the rest of the decade – was Chancellor of the Exchequer; James Callaghan was Foreign Secretary; Roy Jenkins was Home Secretary and the veteran left-winger Michael Foot was Secretary for Employment. Wilson knew that with no overall majority, his government was hanging by a thread; but he also knew he could call an election when the timing felt right.

Yet from the start Wilson gave the impression of a man marking time – perhaps because he had on his mind not only an imminent second general election, but also his long-planned retirement from front-line politics. He was dogged by spurious rumours that he had links with the KGB and was in thrall to his political secretary, Marcia Williams. And he gave the impression of a consummate politician drawing on well-honed skills to muddle on as best he could, rather than someone bursting with ideas and energy, ready to tackle the nation's economic crisis. In effect, his premiership settled for reducing the patient's fever rather than radical surgery. In the circumstances, perhaps that was the best that could be done.

The new Labour government pinned much of its hope on the Social Contract with the unions, and it started dynamically enough. Within 48 hours of taking office the government had settled with the miners, who accepted a 35 per cent pay increase. The power cuts came to an end, along with the three-day week. Then, also in March, Denis Healey implemented an emergency budget that hiked up taxation, VAT and petrol duty, but also increased pensions and introduced food subsidies. Healey likened the economy to the Augean Stables of Ancient Greek myth – in the tale of the Twelve Labours of Hercules, the fifth of his tasks was to clean the stables of King Augeas in a single day.

Spring shake up

The sudden spurt of political action allowed the public to breath a collective sigh of relief. The underlying problems of industrial unrest, unemployment and inflation may not have gone away, but the sense of immediate crisis was over. The daily newspapers and the nightly TV bulletins could at last replace government spokesmen and miners leaders with news of other events.

One such event that literally changed the map of Britain was the Local Government Act, which came into effect on 1 April, 1974. Many hoped it was an elaborate April Fool's joke, because the Act

BACK IN THE HOT SEAT
After re-election, Harold Wilson – shown here (right) in 1974, talking to the press at Transport House in London – never really impressed either his party or the country with his old sense of leadership. He remained Prime Minister for two years, winning a fourth general election in October 1974, before retiring. His colleague Roy Jenkins would later write: 'The weakness of the second Wilson government was essentially that, having achieved the object for which he had suffered much obloquy and punishment, that of walking back through the front door of 10 Downing Street in his own right, his next central objective became that of walking out again as soon as … he responsibly could.'

In fact, by the time of his resignation in March 1976 Harold Wilson may already have been feeling early symptoms of the Alzheimer's Disease that before long would start to rob him of his formidable intellect and memory. On his retirement, the Queen showed her personal appreciation of her departing Prime Minister by dining with the Wilsons before they left Downing Street.

created new local administrative authorities and abolished many others. Rutland, England's smallest county, for example, was subsumed into Leicestershire and disappeared. Some neighbouring counties, like Herefordshire and Worcestershire, were yoked together. New county names appeared on the map of England, such as Avon and the West Midlands, a metropolitan county encompassing Birmingham, Coventry and Wolverhampton. The many shires of Wales – Flintshire, Radnorshire, Caernarfonshire, to name but three – were swallowed up by huge new counties such as Clwyd, Gwynedd and Powys. The following year a similar Act came into force in Scotland, and ancient county names redolent of history, such as Clackmannan and Ardnamurchan, were parcelled up into prosaically labelled regions, such as Central and Highland.

Although the spring saw political and administrative changes in the UK, it was business as usual in the troubled province of Northern Ireland. Those opposed to the Northern Ireland Assembly had won 11 out of 12 seats in the general election. And when the Assembly still showed support for the Sunningdale Agreement on 14 May, 1974, the Ulster Workers' Council – a grouping of Protestant trade unions – called for a general strike. For the next two weeks the province ground to a halt. Silent factories, power cuts, food shortages, uncollected rubbish and angry protests took their toll on the Stormont government. On 28 May, Brian Faulkner and the pro-agreement Unionists resigned. Merlyn Rees, the Northern Ireland Secretary, immediately reimposed direct rule from Westminster.

LET US PLAY
Sir Alf Ramsey delivers a team talk at the England training ground at Stevenage, in Hertfordshire, in May 1973. Beside him facing the players is his captain, Bobby Moore. The year 1973 was a watershed for the England team and for Ramsey: in October that year they lost to Poland and with that defeat failed to qualify for the 1974 World Cup. The result spelled the end for Ramsey as manager. In the decade he had been in charge, England won 69 of their matches, drew 27 and lost just 17. But the times were changing. The reserved, almost aloof Ramsey had the respect of both fans and players, but he seemed almost of another era, out of place among the younger, more extrovert and media-savvy managers of the day. He remained in football, managing Birmingham City until 1978. He died in 1999 at the age of 79.

Winners and losers

On the evening of 6 April, 1974, as Britons gathered around their TV sets to see how Olivia Newton-John would fare with 'Long Live Love' in the Eurovision Song Contest, they and the rest of Europe got their first sight of Abba. The group's assured performance of 'Waterloo' won them the contest, but few could have suspected at the time that they would come to dominate the charts in Britain and around the world. 'Waterloo' was the first of nine number one hits for ABBA in the UK and their music has never really gone away.

If Abba brought a splash of colour and vitality into Britain that spring, it failed to touch the English football team which was utterly in the doldrums. In 1973 they had failed to qualify for the World Cup. Needing to beat Poland at Wembley they did everything but score, not least because of an inspired performance by the Polish goalkeeper. The failure put Ramsey's head on the block and in May 1974 the FA's axe fell. In retrospect, it seemed to many that Sir Alf's enforced departure heralded an era of sustained English failure at international level, with a procession of managers – Joe Mercer, Don Revie, Ron Greenwood – unable to coax the team to any notable achievements.

> ## '[It was] the most devastating half-hour of my life … I stood in a room almost full of staring committee men. It was just like I was on trial. I thought I was going to be hanged.'
>
> Alf Ramsey, on the experience of being sacked as England manager in 1974

North of the border, in contrast, there was much celebration and not just because of England's embarrassment. Scotland did qualify for the World Cup finals that year and a tartan army of fans travelled to West Germany to support their team. If the fans were disappointed, it was not the fault of the Scottish team, who performed valiantly. At the end of the group stage they were on equal points with Yugoslavia and Brazil, but they were knocked out on goal difference having conceded just one goal – it was one more than Brazil.

The October election

During the pleasant summer of 1974 the government managed to steer clear of damaging disasters and in September, with opinion polls favourable, Wilson announced a general election to be held on 10 October. Campaigning was low-key and somewhat lacking in passion, just as it had been for the election earlier in the year. The Tories, with Heath still at the helm, were a party desperately in need of a change of direction. Labour played it safe, seeking to persuade voters of the benefits of their partnership with the unions.

In the end, Labour's victory was unconvincing. They gained an overall majority, but of just three seats. The margin might have been better had the

LABOUR SCEPTICS
The issue of whether Britain should remain in the EEC split opinion within political parties and made some unlikely alliances. In April 1975 Labour held a party conference to debate the issue. Harold Wilson was unequivocal, declaring that: 'It is now best for the future of Britain, best for the Commonwealth, best for the developing world, best for the wider world, that we remain in the Community.' It made no difference to the Labour delegates at the conference: the anti-Europe side won by a majority of almost 2 votes to 1. Prominent among Labour's anti-group were the Industry Secretary Tony Benn and the Trade Secretary Peter Shore, seen here (left, wearing glasses) at a referendum press conference in May 1975.

Scottish Nationalists not enjoyed a breakthrough election, winning a record 11 seats at Westminster. With his time as leader running out, Heath pronounced his hope that Labour would acknowledge that 60 per cent of the voters were 'against the policies of socialism'. Wilson tried to rise above party politics, declaring that 'in the wider national interest … Parliament should give a lead to the country'. He made no bones about the dire state of the nation: 'Britain faces, and has for some considerable time been facing, the gravest economic crisis since the war.'

Referendum on Europe

A central plank of Labour's campaign was the promise of a referendum to let the people decide whether the country should stay in the EEC or withdraw. While this was being organised, the Labour government would renegotiate Britain's terms with Europe, including its budgetary contribution. As 1974 slipped into 1975, the referendum was hardly out of the news. People were amused to see old foes burying their various hatchets to argue the case for or against EEC membership. Heavyweights on the pro-side included Heath and Margaret Thatcher – elected party leader in February 1975 (see page 85) – who lined up with Labour's Wilson, Healey and Jenkins and the Liberal leader Jeremy Thorpe. On the anti side, Enoch Powell – now Ulster Unionist MP for South Down – made a strange bedfellow for Labour left-wingers Tony Benn, Peter Shore and Michael Foot, who were joined by the Scottish Nationalists and some Tory backbenchers.

At an EEC summit held in Dublin in March 1975, Britain's budgetary contribution terms were modified. Little else changed in the arrangements with Europe, but Harold Wilson seemed reasonably content with the outcome. Then, on 5 June, the people of Britain went to the polls to answer the question: 'Do you think the UK should stay in the European Community (Common Market)?' The result was not even close. Some 17 million voted to stay, with 8 million against, showing that most were persuaded that the country's best interest lay with Europe. Wilson expressed himself delighted with the people's 'historic decision'.

THE BIG COUNT
Votes in the referendum on Europe being counted at Earl's Court Exhibition Centre in London on 6 June, 1975 (right). The result was a resounding endorsement of Britain's EEC membership, with two thirds of voters being in favour. This came as an enormous relief to pro-Europe MPs on both the Labour and Conservative benches. The Home Secretary Roy Jenkins commented that the vote ended the uncertainty, committing Britain to 'playing an active, constructive and enthusiastic role' in Europe. For Ted Heath it was a vindication of 25 years hard work. On the losing side, the anti-EEC Tony Benn accepted defeat with good grace: 'When the British people speak, everyone, including members of Parliament, should tremble before their decision and that's certainly the spirit with which I accept the result of the referendum.'

THE POLARISING OF POLITICS

BIG BENN
Much of the energy that drove the radical Labour left in the Seventies emanated from Tony Benn. Born in 1925, Benn became MP for Bristol Southeast in 1950. In 1963 he renounced the peerage he had inherited from his father in order to remain an MP. Under Harold Wilson's first government (1964–70) Benn became Postmaster General then Minister of Technology, gaining a reputation for committed socialist views. In Wilson's second government, he served as Industry Secretary. In 1976 Benn stood in the leadership contest that followed Wilson's resignation, but he attracted relatively few votes. He remained the darling of local activists and continued to argue passionately for his socialist vision, which included greater democracy within Labour, nationalisation of industry, withdrawal from the EEC and abolition of the House of Lords.

In the mid-1970s, there was a distinct regrouping by the political left and right. Wilson and Heath had both occupied the centre ground, unwilling to sacrifice pragmatism and consensus politics on the altar of ideology. But despite their well-meaning endeavours, the country was in a mess, and the opposing forces of both left and right were champing at the bit to recast the nation in their own images. Harold Wilson now found he had to deal not only with the country's problems but also with the radical left in his own party, for whom the Industry Secretary Tony Benn was the natural leader.

A charismatic and tenacious ideologue, Benn sought to drive through an alternative industrial policy. His brand of socialism envisaged a Britain with more public ownership, a National Enterprise Board that had the power to buy failing firms, and economic planning agreements with the trade unions. In effect, industrial responsibility would be split three ways between the government, the employers and the workers. Far from being part of a 'loony left' strategy, Benn's broad plan was part of Labour's official policy: on 15 August, 1974, the government had published a White Paper in preparation for an Industry Bill to put such socialist policies into practice.

But Wilson baulked at medicine he believed would be rejected by the patient. With only a three-seat majority he felt he could not afford to antagonise an electorate that was clearly perturbed by union power. In addition, an alarmed CBI (Confederation of British Industry) repeatedly expressed grave concern about the Industry Bill to Wilson in person. Benn, already a hate figure for the right-wing press, was too influential and charismatic to sack. So Wilson 'emasculated' (to use the left-wing MP Ian Mikardo's word) the bill with amendments. Then in May 1975, just before the referendum – Benn believed membership of the EEC was ruinous to Britain's interest – Wilson removed him from his post at Industry and let him cool his heels in the less influential Energy department.

Thwarted by his boss and isolated in Cabinet, Benn had to lick his wounds and wait for a more propitious moment to promote his agenda. But he made it clear that the policy he was advocating was one that the Labour Party had backed in conference. Therein lay the snag. For left-wingers it was a constant source of frustration that decisions made at party conferences – where trade unions wielded huge block votes – were routinely ignored or toned down by the parliamentary party. In other words, many Labour MPs – and especially the leadership – were out of sympathy with the radical left views of party workers and trade unionists.

THE HARD LEFT

By mid-decade, both the Conservative and Labour parties were witnessing ideological struggles on their right and left wings respectively. Harold Wilson and Ted Heath were essentially one-nation politicians, constantly seeking unity in the centre ground, which inevitably entailed compromise. The Labour left argued for more radical socialist policies than Wilson and most of his Cabinet colleagues were prepared to pursue. Dennis Skinner (left), who was first elected MP for Bolsover in 1970, was an ex-miner who personified the honest, left-wing socialist. The press would soon nickname him the 'Beast of Bolsover'. Ricky Tomlinson (below right) was a trade union activist before starting the acting career that would make him a household name.

Militants of the left

Outside the Labour Party, left-wing radicals and would-be revolutionaries were drawn to the Socialist Workers Party and the Workers Revolutionary Party, the political home of thespians Vanessa and Corin Redgrave. But even at grassroots level within the Labour Party, there were ultra-left militants agitating for a greater say in the running of the party. Militant Tendency, a Trotskyist-inspired movement, infiltrated local Labour branches with the aim of gaining positions on general management committees.

This covert 'entryism' into Labour worked – especially in Liverpool – and by the mid-1970s Militant was beginning to wield significant influence. Its most high-profile success came in the summer of 1975 when the veteran Labour MP Reg Prentice found himself deselected in his London constituency of Newham Northeast. Not even a petition of 180 Labour MPs could save him. Labour's National Executive Committee upheld the deselection, and Prentice's personal appeal at the October 1976 party conference bore no fruit. The following year he crossed the floor and joined the Conservatives. Militant would continue to be a thorn in the flesh of Labour leaders until the mid-1980s, when a get-tough policy resulted in Militant members being expelled from the party.

Tory renewal

The Conservatives were about to embark on an ideological revolution of the right. After their election defeat in October 1974, it was clear to most Tories that Ted Heath had to go. He had led the party with dignity, but while defeat in two elections could be regarded as unfortunate, the third branded him a loser. As the party considered its options, the most significant figure to emerge in the public eye was Sir Keith Joseph, a member of the shadow cabinet. A sensitive intellectual from a wealthy Jewish background, Joseph conducted a root-and-branch review of Conservative policy and, during the summer of 1974, he confronted his party's failure on the economy in a series of compelling speeches.

Joseph's main arguments were that the country should embrace the free market and that the money supply should be reined in to create greater economic stability, even at the risk of unemployment. He attacked Britain's high levels of public spending, high taxes, nationalisation of industries and the union-dominated culture that held back enterprise. In short, he summed up what would become known as monetarism – and, later, Thatcherism.

His evangelical fervour went down well with the Tories and Joseph became their man of the moment, the front-runner to succeed Heath. He then made a fatal error. On 19 October, 1974, just after the election, he delivered a speech that included an emotional diatribe about young, working-class, single mothers who produced 'problem children, the future unmarried mothers, delinquents'. The killer statement was when he declared: 'The balance of our population, our human stock is threatened.' He was immediately accused of advocating eugenics. Joe Gormley, the miners' leader, crudely interpreted Joseph's message as 'we should put down

POINTING TO THE RIGHT
Sir Keith Joseph – shown here making a speech at a Conservative Party conference in Brighton – was a brilliant intellectual who many tipped to succeed Ted Heath as leader of the Conservatives. Born in 1918, Joseph fought in Italy in the Second World War, where he read Shakespeare in Italian to teach himself the language. In 1946 he became a prize fellow at All Souls College, Oxford. He was elected to Parliament in 1956 as MP for Leeds Northeast and quickly established himself as a politician of integrity and new ideas. In 1974 he co-founded, with Alfred Sherman, the Centre for Policy Studies, the think tank that would become the Tory seminary of liberal economics and monetarism. They were joined at the CPS by Margaret Thatcher.

'We are over-governed, over-spent, over-taxed, over-borrowed and over-manned.'

Sir Keith Joseph, on the problems of Britain's economy in 1974

the kids produced by what he calls the lower classes'. Although Joseph quickly realised his mistake, it was too late – he was damaged goods. He withdrew from the leadership contest and urged his friend Margaret Thatcher to run instead.

Making history

Mrs Thatcher was cut from very different cloth to Keith Joseph. Born in Grantham in Lincolnshire, she was raised in a middle-class household that valued hard work, enterprise and thrift. Her father was a grocer and also a local alderman and Methodist lay preacher. Thatcher won a place at Oxford University to read chemistry and later trained as a barrister. She entered Parliament in 1959 as the Conservative MP for Finchley. In 1970 Edward Heath appointed her Secretary of State for Education and Science, during which time she ended free school milk, inspiring the chant 'Margaret Thatcher, Milk Snatcher'.

Thatcher was an unlikely challenger to Heath. For a start, there had never been a woman leader of a major political party in Britain. She was one of very few women in a political sea of men and the press were unable to resist patronising comments, focusing more on her clothes and hats than her policies. And then there was her image: her plummy voice and prim manner made her seem to many more like an organiser for the Women's Institute than a potential Prime Minister.

On 4 February, 1975, Heath bowed to the inevitable and called for a party leadership election. In the first ballot, Thatcher stood against Heath and the backbencher Hugh Fraser. Much to everyone's surprise, Thatcher beat Heath by 130 votes to 119, and Heath resigned his position as leader. But the contest was

OUT WITH THE OLD
Ted Heath hung on as leader of the Conservatives for almost a year after losing the election of February 1974. The pressure on him grew after losing again in October 1974. When he consented to a leadership challenge, he had no inkling that his most serious rival would be Margaret Thatcher. This photograph shows them together in October 1970 at the Conservative Party conference, when he was Prime Minister and she was Education Secretary in the Tory Cabinet. Thatcher's campaign for the party leadership was masterminded by the experienced back-bencher Airey Neave, who gathered support for her behind the scenes. Following her victory, her tendency to adopt right-wing economic policies soon alienated Heath. After Mrs Thatcher became Prime Minister in 1979, he turned down her offer to appoint him as Britain's ambassador in Washington.

not yet over. In a second ballot, held on 11 February, Thatcher came up against Willie Whitelaw, a leading Heath loyalist. She won decisively by 146 to 79 votes. She had become the first female leader of the Conservative Party. When asked whether she would be celebrating, she replied: 'Good heavens, no. There's far too much work to be done', thereby setting the tone for the Thatcher years ahead in the 1980s. Edward du Cann, then chairman of the influential 1922 backbench committee, declared: 'We have a new and rather exciting leader. Mrs Thatcher will make the Tory Party distinctive.' How right he was.

Beyond politics

Economic issues and politics never went away in 1975, but they were sometimes pushed off the front page. In February, London Underground suffered one of its worst disasters when a tube train crashed at Moorgate station, claiming 43 lives. The cause of the accident was a mystery. The driver, who was killed, had been in good health, but for some unaccountable reason had failed to apply the brakes.

The summer brought welcome diversion and not-so-welcome drama for cricket-lovers in the form of the Ashes Test series against Australia. The third Test at Headingley in Leeds, with England gaining supremacy, had to be abandoned after the wicket was vandalised – not by political activists, but by supporters of a London minicab driver named George Davis who had been jailed for armed

FAREWELL GRAHAM HILL
A policeman surveys the wreckage of Graham Hill's Piper Aztec plane following the crash near Arkley golf course in Hertfordshire in which Hill and five members of his team all died in November 1975. Visibility at the time of the crash had been extremely poor – one golf club member said that 'the ambulances couldn't even see the bunkers as they were driving down'. The loss of racing driver Graham Hill was felt keenly by many. He was a popular, larger-than-life personality, recognised up and down the land. He had begun his Formula One career in 1958 and won the drivers' championship twice, in 1962 and 1968. He retired from racing in July 1975. He is still the only driver to have won all three of the big racing trophies – the Indianapolis 500, the 24-hour Le Mans and the Formula One World Championship.

robbery. Campaigners claimed that he was a victim of mistaken identity. Davis was released in May 1976, but two years later he pleaded guilty to bank robbery and was jailed for 15 years. Australia went on to win the four-match series 1-0.

Autumn 1975 saw the unexpected deaths of Ross McWhirter and Graham Hill. McWhirter was a TV presenter and co-author, with his twin brother Norris, of the *Guinness Book of Records*. He was also an outspoken critic of the IRA. On 27 November, he was gunned down by Irish republicans at the front door of his home in North London. Two days later Graham Hill, one of Britain's greatest racing drivers, died in a plane crash. He had been piloting his light aircraft in dense fog when he clipped trees on a golf course.

November did bring some cheer to the country, and a welcome boost to the Labour government's morale, when the Queen formally opened the UK's first North Sea oil pipeline. In time, the oil would do much to help the country's energy needs and balance of payments – but not just yet. As 1975 ended, the government seemed becalmed. Even the unions were becoming concerned at the high level of wage claims. The TUC endorsed a plan, put forward by Jack Jones, for voluntary wage restraint. Austerity was in the air. As the Environment Secretary Anthony Crosland had commented earlier in the year: 'The party is over.'

UNDERGROUND CATASTROPHE
A policeman guides passengers along a platform at Moorgate station 10 days after the worst crash in the history of London Underground. At the height of the morning rush hour, a train jammed with office-workers and other commuters sped past the platform and crashed into the dead-end tunnel. The front three carriages were crushed together leaving three behind intact. The station was plunged into darkness and rescue workers had to contend with clouds of dust and soot before confronting what one journalist described as 'a horrible mess of limbs and mangled iron'. An inquiry found that the track, signals and train were all in good working order. It failed to establish the cause of the crash or why the driver Leslie Newson had not applied the brakes in time.

PUNK AND THE JUBILEE

As the curtain rose on January 1976 people were humming Queen's Christmas hit, 'Bohemian Rhapsody', with its striking opening lines: 'Is this the real life? Is this just fantasy?' Many must have wished the troubles in Northern Ireland were a fantasy, as real life in the province descended into a nightmare of tit-for-tat violence. On 5 January, a minibus was ambushed in Armagh and ten Protestant textile workers were shot dead. The massacre was believed to be in retaliation for the killing of five Catholics the night before. Later in the month, the IRA detonated twelve bombs in London, including one in Selfridge's in Oxford Street. Luckily, the explosions were during the night, and there was only one casualty.

HAIR RAISING CHANGE In 1976 Punk took off in Britain, starting a fad for spectacular Mohican hair cuts (left) and changing music and style for good.

PLANET MERCURY

The pop charts of Christmas 1975 were dominated by Queen as 'Bohemian Rhapsody', sung by the flamboyant Freddie Mercury (left), held the number one slot for nine weeks. It became the third highest-selling single of all time. Queen came to prominence in the early Seventies, combining Mercury's camp showmanship and operatic vocals with solid rock music and Brian May's distinctive lead guitar. In 1974 they had a smash hit in the UK and in America with 'Killer Queen', but it was the album *A Night at the Opera*, released in 1975, that took them to global stardom. Queen flourished until Mercury's death, from AIDS, in 1991. They have now clocked up more than 300 million album sales.

ARTISTRY ON ICE

Britain scored a rare sporting triumph at the Winter Olympics on 11 February, 1976, when the figure skater John Curry (right) won gold in Austria. The 26-year-old Brummie impressed the judges as well as the huge audience with his balletic style, perfect triple jumps and sublime interpretation of the music. A month later he won the World Championships – the first Briton to do so for nearly 40 years, and only the second British winner ever. Later in the year the British public showed their appreciation by voting him BBC Sports Personality of the Year. Curry retired from championship skating soon after and formed an ice dance troupe which put on spectacular shows. The photograph shows him rehearsing for his show at the Cambridge Theatre in December 1976.

February 1976 brought the welcome fantasy world of the Winter Olympics onto Britain's television screens from Innsbruck in Austria. The nation lapped up the reflected glory of John Curry, who won a gold medal in figure skating. Not only was it Britain's first gold medal in the event, it was the first medal of any sort won by Britain at a Winter Olympics for 12 years. Curry thrilled the 10,000-strong crowd and millions of TV viewers with his artistic performance, combining perfectly executed balletic jumps with a sensitive interpretation of the music.

CHANGE AT THE TOP

On 16 March, 1976, Harold Wilson shocked the nation – and his Cabinet – by announcing his resignation. Wilson had led the Labour Party for 13 years and the country for eight of those. He had seemed an indispensable part of the British establishment, a political survivor who would go on and on. But it was not to be. He later claimed that he had made up his mind in 1974 to leave office after his 60th birthday, which he celebrated on 11 March.

Wilson's departure was made controversial by a resignation honours list – the so-called 'Lavender List' – that included 'some adventurous business gentlemen', to borrow Roy Jenkins' decorous phrase. But first and foremost it meant a change of Labour leader and Prime Minister. After three ballots, James Callaghan came out on top, defeating in the process Michael Foot and Denis Healey.

Enter Sunny Jim
Born in Portsmouth, Callaghan grew up in a naval family and was nicknamed 'Sailor Jim' (as well as 'Sunny Jim' for his smiley disposition). His father died when he was nine and thenceforth he was heavily influenced by his mother, who brought him up as a Baptist. Callaghan entered politics not via the time-honoured route of the Oxford or Cambridge Union but through his involvement in trade unions. He took his seat in Parliament in 1945, representing Cardiff South, and then inexorably rose up the Labour Party ranks. Unflappable, clever and politically adroit, he eventually became the first man ever to hold all four great offices of state: Prime Minister, Chancellor, Foreign Secretary and Home Secretary.

Labour was not the only party to require a change of leader that year. On 9 May, Jeremy Thorpe resigned as leader of the Liberal Party after being associated with a scandal involving an ex-male model named Norman Scott. In October 1975 Scott had nearly been shot by a 'hit man' named Andrew Newton. At Newton's trial in 1976, Scott claimed to have had a homosexual relationship with Thorpe, who had no choice but to stand down. Jo Grimond, Thorpe's predecessor as Liberal leader, stepped in while a new permanent leader was found. The choice eventually fell on 38-year-old David Steel, who easily defeated his main rival, John Pardoe. A native of Fife and a law graduate from Edinburgh University, Steel brought a fresh, youthful dynamism to the Liberals.

The IMF crisis

Callaghan immediately set about putting his own stamp on his first Cabinet. He sacked Barbara Castle and replaced Roy Jenkins as Foreign Secretary with Tony Crosland. Jenkins left the government and Parliament altogether, taking refuge in his beloved Europe and becoming President of the European Commission.

Callaghan's most pressing problem was the economy. Inflation, the bugbear of the decade, was on the rise, but so was unemployment. The Bank of England had been spending immoderate sums of money propping up sterling, which had had an unhealthy reputation for some time – not helped by an article entitled 'Good-bye, Great Britain' published in the *Wall Street Journal* in April 1975,

JIM'LL FIX IT

Jim Callaghan did his best to unite the Labour Party. In his acceptance speech as leader and Prime Minister, he appealed to the Tribune and Manifesto groups of the party, representing the left and right respectively, to stop squabbling and 'wipe the slate clean'. One of the gripes of the left was the government's spending on military weapons while cuts were being made in education and other domestic concerns. In October 1976, after laying a foundation stone for an extension of Ruskin College, Oxford (below), he gave a passionate speech defending Labour's record on education. 'The goals of our education are clear enough', he claimed. 'They are to equip children to the best of their ability for a lively, constructive place in society, and also to fit them to do a job of work. Not one or the other but both.'

which advised investors to jettison sterling. As spring turned to summer, Chancellor Denis Healey realised that the country needed a multi-billion loan from the International Monetary Fund (IMF) to survive. He also knew that the IMF would impose strict fiscal conditions that the unions would not like.

The crisis then accelerated. On 28 September, 1976, the day after the Labour Party conference had begun, Healey went to Heathrow for a flight to New York where he was to meet with IMF officials. As he was waiting to board the plane, the pound deteriorated so suddenly he had to return to No.11 to manage the crisis. It was a PR disaster.

In a landmark speech at the conference, Callaghan spelled out the reality of the hard times ahead and announced a radical change in government thinking. Keynesian economics, with its ideal of full employment through government intervention, was no longer the way forward: 'We used to think that you could just spend your way out of a recession and increase employment by cutting taxes and boosting government spending. I tell you, in all candour, that that option no longer exists and that in so far as it ever did exist, it only worked on each occasion since the war by injecting bigger doses of inflation into the economy, followed by higher levels of unemployment.' When Healey addressed the conference on 30 September to announce strict economic measures, he was booed from the stage.

Over the next months, Britain duly went 'cap-in-hand' to the IMF for a loan. An IMF delegation arrived in Britain in November and laid down the law about cuts in public spending. In fact, it later turned out that through a miscalculation the public sector borrowing requirement was much less than was thought necessary, and so the IMF-mandated cuts were more brutal than they need have been.

Then, slowly but surely, the economy started to right itself. In the first half of 1977 sterling and the financial markets began to recover and unemployment fell. Nevertheless, the image of Britain being bailed out by the IMF like some third-world banana republic had damaged the country's international reputation, as well as the Labour government's claim to economic competence.

Happy days

In complete contrast to the gloom and doom of politics and the economy, many people were actually having a good time in 1976. For a start there was the long hot summer, which transformed Britain's drab streets with Mediterranean sunshine (see pages 106-9). There were also magic moments of success. In the Montreal Olympics, Scottish swimmer David Wilkie powered to gold in the 200 metres breaststroke – Britain's first swimming gold medal for 68 years. Then on 24 October James Hunt won the Formula One motor-racing world championship. The blond, charismatic Hunt needed to overhaul his rival Niki Lauda in the last race of the season in Japan. In torrential conditions Lauda was forced to retire from the race, while Hunt came in third to beat the Austrian by one point.

DOES IT HURT?
Denis Healey receives some painful attention from his grandson in March 1977. As Chancellor, Healey steered the country through the IMF crisis, but not without difficult moments. When a sudden drop in the value of the pound forced him to turn back from Heathrow airport and abandon a meeting with the IMF in New York, it was not just the markets that reacted badly. Healey would later write: 'It was the lowest point of my period at the Treasury. For the first and last time in my life, for about twelve hours I was close to demoralisation.' He also wrote of how he looked forward to 'sod off day' – the day when the loan had been fully repaid to the IMF.

The day after Hunt's triumph, one of the longest-running sagas in the history of theatre-building came to an end when the Queen opened the National Theatre on London's South Bank, 25 years after laying the foundation stone at the Festival Hall. Designed by Sir Denys Lasdun, the concrete complex was not to everyone's taste – Prince Charles described it as 'a clever way of building a nuclear power station in the middle of London without anyone objecting' – but, for better or worse, it was now the home of the National Theatre Company, formerly based at the Old Vic. After fireworks and fanfares, Sir Laurence Olivier gave a welcoming speech in the auditorium that bore his name (the other two, yet to be completed, would be the Lyttelton and Cottesloe theatres), and the Queen was treated to a performance of *Il Campiello* by 18th-century Venetian playwright Carlo Goldoni.

GOLDEN BOYS

Scottish swimmer David Wilkie (above) lit up Britain's hot summer of 1976 by taking gold in the 200 metres breaststroke at the Montreal Olympics. Wilkie had also won silver at the Munich Olympics in 1972.

The country was more accustomed to success in motor racing, but it was still a thrill to see a new British world champion. The blond, dashing ex-public schoolboy James Hunt drew new viewers to Formula One in the first half of the 1970s with his fearless driving and fun-loving playboy image. His biggest moment of glory came in 1976 when he finished third in appalling conditions in Japan (far right) to win the drivers' championship for the first and only time. Here he is celebrating his victory in the Race of Champions at Brands Hatch in 1977 (right). Hunt retired from racing in 1979 and eventually became a motor-racing commentator for the BBC. He died of a heart attack in 1993 aged just 45.

MAESTRO OF PUNK

In 1976 and 1977 the Sex Pistols, under the canny guidance of their manager Malcolm McLaren (right), made themselves synonymous with Punk. The band evolved from a group called The Strand, which McLaren had managed since the early Seventies. In 1975 he added John Lydon, aka Johnny Rotten, to the line-up as lead singer and they changed their name to the Sex Pistols. By the next year, they had a cult following. In December 1976 they embarked on their Anarchy in the UK tour (above) with the Damned, Johnny Thunders' Heartbreakers and the Clash. McLaren's promotion for the tour was given a huge boost by a media frenzy following the use of the F-word by one of the band in a notorious TV interview on Thames Television. The *Daily Mirror* ran a front-page headline 'The Filth and the Fury', claiming 'Uproar as viewers jam phones'. For anyone who had missed it, the article reported: 'A pop group shocked millions of viewers last night with the filthiest language heard on British television.' It was bad news for the interviewer, Bill Grundy, who was suspended by Thames, but for the Sex Pistols it was the sort of publicity money could not buy.

WAKING UP TO PUNK

VICIOUS CIRCLE
Simon John Ritchie, aka Sid Vicious (below), joined the Sex Pistols in early 1977 and played on the notorious 'God Save the Queen' single. Despite – or perhaps because of – a BBC ban, the song reached No.2 in the official UK charts. To add insult to monarchist injury, on the Jubilee weekend itself the band chartered a boat (which they named the *Queen Elizabeth*) and sailed it past the Houses of Parliament with their music blaring from loud speakers. They were pursued by the police and arrested. For a brief while, the Pistols were the hottest, most outrageous band on the planet, but success was short-lived. Young Britain might have been ready for their tidal wave of riotous change, but the USA was not. Hostile audiences, bad planning and divisive tensions within the band all took their toll on the US tour of 1978.

By late 1976, Punk rock had arrived – it was loud, brash, refreshingly simplistic and stuck two fingers up at most manifestations of the Establishment. Musically, Punk fulfilled a need to get back to a primitive core of sound, stripped of what its musicians and fans saw as the pretentiousness of progressive rock, the vacuous glitter of Glam and the inanity of disco. The nuclear Punk band consisted of just bass and rhythm guitars, drums and vocals. It was said that three chords were all you needed. Guitar solos were minimal. The default sound was a raunchy, driving rhythm, over which the lead singer bawled out a torrent of words.

Punk was the expression of a new generation who were thoroughly bored with the hippy ideals and music of the late Sixties and early Seventies. It screamed out anarchy, violence and nihilism, and spawned a new culture proclaimed in shredded clothes, body piercing, shaven heads and garish Mohican hair-cuts.

Shooting first – the Sex Pistols

In the UK the Sex Pistols, fronted by Johnny Rotten, were the first high-profile Punk band to blaze a trail for others to follow, notably the Clash and the Damned. Dressed in ripped jeans and T-shirts held together with safety pins, with garishly dyed, dishevelled hair, the Pistols were out to shock both on and off stage – and they succeeded. In a notorious episode broadcast live on Thames Television on 1 December, 1976, the guitarist Steve Jones told television presenter Bill Grundy he was 'a dirty f***er'. Complaints poured in.

The mastermind behind the Sex Pistols was Malcolm McLaren, entrepreneur, musician and close friend of the Punk fashion designer Vivienne Westwood. The band performed their first gigs in late 1975 at low-key college venues in London. They gradually built up a cult following, including Siouxsie Sioux and Billy Idol, who would achieve fame with Punk bands of their own (Siouxsie and the Banshees and Generation X respectively). In early 1976 the Pistols graduated to more prestigious venues in London, such as the 100 Club on New Oxford Street, and in June they stormed Manchester's Lesser Free Trade Hall with a gig that lit the fires of Punk in the north. Soon they had support acts such as the Clash and the Damned, and their first major UK tour took place in the autumn.

The music industry was beginning to take the Pistols seriously. In October 1976, EMI took the plunge and signed them up. The first single, 'Anarchy in the UK', was released in late November. Full of high-octane energy and venomous attitude, the song set out its stall in the first two lines: 'I am an antichrist/ I am an anarchist.' Although the record stalled at number 38 in the UK charts, its influence would resonate down the years.

The relationship with EMI did not last long. The band were dropped in January 1977 because of their obscene behaviour. In March, A&M Records tried their luck, but just ten days after signing the band, the record company terminated the contract following a particularly riotous and destructive party in A&M's offices. Two months later the Pistols signed up with Virgin Records, who released their second single, 'God Save the Queen', on the 27 May – timed to coincide with the height of the Queen's Jubilee celebrations. Branded by the group as an alternative national anthem, the song was a mixture of anti-royalist, anarchist and nihilist lyrics that caused maximum offence. They split the country between the outraged and the amused. The Sex Pistols exposed the generation gap like no other band before or since. The Beatles they certainly were not.

But the sensationalism of the band was a double-edged sword. Publicity flowed from their antics, but music venues and insurance companies became increasingly wary of them and the wreckage they left strewn in their wake. By the autumn of 1977 the Pistols were forced to go on their UK tour in secret, adopting pseudonyms to prevent them being banned by the venues. Their decline was rapid,

HIGH PRIESTESS OF PUNK
Vivienne Westwood (above) was a former arts student who opened a boutique called 'Sex' on the Kings Road, Chelsea, with Malcolm McLaren. The shop advertised itself as 'specialists in rubberwear, glamourwear and stagewear' and featured Westwood's flamboyant designs, leather and rubber bondage gear, T-shirts with slogans, spiked dog collars, chains and other Punk accoutrements. Her creations were showcased by the Sex Pistols, and she became acknowledged as an original trendsetter. In an extraordinary reflection of how taste and perceptions change, in 2006 she was made a Dame of the British Empire in recognition of her services to fashion.

NEW DIRECTION
Three of the Sex Pistols – left to right, Sid Vicious, Paul Cook on drums and Johnny Rotten – in June 1977. The original bass player, Glen Matlock, left the band in early 1977 because of 'differences' – reasons suggested for his departure included that he 'liked the Beatles' and 'washed his feet'. His replacement was Simon John Ritchie, better known as

Sid Vicious, who to begin with could not play guitar, but he had the look and the attitude in spades. He took the band to new heights – or depths – of outrage. But he was out of his depth himself. With his American girlfriend Nancy Spungen, he descended into a spiral of heroin addiction and violence, that led first to her death and then, early in 1979, to his own. By then, the Sex Pistols had ceased to be.

beginning in January 1978 on a disastrous US tour. Johnny Rotten was frustrated by his vain attempts to fire McLaren and he left the group, effectively bringing about its demise. Meanwhile, Sid Vicious was on a downward spiral of heroin-addiction. On 12 October his junkie girlfriend Nancy Spungen was found dead, stabbed in the stomach, in their hotel room in New York. Vicious was arrested on suspicion of murder, then released on bail in early 1979. On 2 February that year he died of a heroin overdose, aged just 21.

The Clash and the Damned

The Sex Pistols handed their spittle-drenched baton to the Clash, reckoned to be the second most influential UK Punk band. Formed in 1976, their core line-up consisted of Joe Strummer (the son of a diplomat) on vocals and guitar, Mick Jones on lead guitar, Paul Simonon on bass and Nicky 'Topper' Headon on drums. The Clash had the same energy and verve as the Pistols, but also a greater musical complexity, with influences from reggae, ska, funk, and elsewhere. They were also more politically aware than the Pistols, espousing solid left-wing ideals as opposed to the Pistols' message of mayhem. They still had their run-ins with authority – petty theft and shooting racing pigeons attracted the attention of the police, and an audience riot after one of their gigs in London maintained their punk street cred.

    The Clash played their first gig in July 1976 as support act for the Sex Pistols. By early 1977 they had signed a deal with CBS Records. Their commercial and critical success continued well into the 1980s, but by mid-decade tensions within the band had become irreconcilable and Strummer and Simonon called it a day.

THE CLASH
After the demise of the Sex Pistols, the Clash took Punk rock to another level of musical complexity and commercial success. Fronted by Joe Strummer (right) and guitarist Mick Jones (above), the band signed a lucrative record deal with CBS, prompting music writer Mark Perry to comment: 'Punk died the day The Clash signed to CBS.' Their breakthrough album was *London Calling*, which not only made the top ten in the UK chart in late 1979 but also reached number 27 in the US chart in the following year.

'Were it not for the Clash, punk would have been just a sneer, a safety pin and a pair of bondage trousers.'

Billy Bragg

THE DAMNED
Formed in London in 1976, the Damned consisted of (above, from left to right), Captain Sensible, Brian James, Dave Vanian and Rat Scabies. Vanian, Sensible and Scabies had previously played together in the short-lived Masters of the Backside, alongside Chrissie Hynde, the future lead singer of the Pretenders. The Damned reinvented themselves from hard-core Punks in the Seventies to vaudeville Goths in the Eighties. Although their singles – such as 'New Rose', 'Problem Child' and 'Don't Cry Wolf' – never sold in massive quantities, the group built up a dedicated cult following.

Another band who started out supporting the Sex Pistols and went on to outlast them was the Damned. The Damned have a claim to fame for the number of firsts they achieved – the first Punk band to produce a single ('New Rose'), an album (*Damned Damned Damned*) and to tour America. They were also with a new kind of record company, Stiff Records, an independent label formed by music entrepreneurs Dave Robinson and Jake Rivera. Later, they were the first Punk band to split up and then re-form, and have been through many incarnations since. Their founder members were Dave Vanian on vocals, Captain Sensible (Raymond Burns) on bass, Bryan James on guitar and Rat Scabies (Chris Millar) on drums.

Like the Clash, the Damned displayed a wide spectrum of influences in their music, from garage rock to cabaret. The Damned's time as a Punk group was short-lived. In March 1977 they supported T. Rex on their last tour and then got down to record their second album, *Music for Pleasure*. It bombed and the band split up, later re-forming in various combinations but never again as a primary Punk band. Vanian, with his heavily made-up, ghost-white face and sleek black

MUSIC FOR THE CAUSE

Although the spirit of Punk was essentially anarchistic, it did lend itself to left-wing and social causes, including concerts in aid of Rock Against Racism, one of which was attended by the audience above. The Clash supported the RAR movement, as did the Belfast Punk band Stiff Little Fingers. SLF had another cause to chronicle in their songs, the Troubles of Northern Ireland, which caught the attention of the press on their first album, *Inflammable Material*, released in 1979.

hair, was known for his crooning vocals; and in the early 1980s his vampire image became the cornerstone for the Damned's reincarnation as a goth band.

By the end of the decade the raw Punk movement had more or less blown itself out. The Sex Pistols were gone and the Clash were going commercial. The Damned, the Buzzcocks, Stiff Little Fingers and Sham 69 were in retreat. But the influence of Punk would be far longer lived. It had taken rock music back to basics, allowing a 'new wave' of bands the air to flourish. Ian Dury, Elvis Costello, Dr Feelgood, the Jam, the Boomtown Rats – they had the tempo of Punk but displayed more musical subtlety and mainstream influences, and slicker production values. They also seemed to project less anger: the times were changing and the initial explosion of Punk spleen had dissipated into more gentle ripples.

NEW WAVES IN MUSIC

Ian Dury (far left) and Elvis Costello (left) blended Punk energy with New Wave wit and sophistication. Ian Dury, a polio victim at the age of seven, was an arts school graduate who cut his musician's teeth in the early Seventies with a band called Kilburn & the High Roads. In 1977 he formed the Blockheads and success thereafter came thick and fast with a string of hits that combined driving rhythms and witty rhyming lyrics. 'Sex and Drugs and Rock & Roll', released in 1977, became a definitive anthem of the late Seventies. Elvis Costello, born Declan Patrick MacManus, had a musical father who played with the Joe Loss Orchestra. Sporting a Buddy Holly look, and with a backing band called the Attractions,

Costello began to make waves in 1977 with his first major hit, 'Watching the Detectives'. The Boomtown Rats, fronted by Bob Geldof (bottom left), reached number one in November 1978 with 'Rat Trap'. They matched this the following year with what became their signature song, 'I Don't Like Mondays'. Sham 69, fronted by Jimmy Pursey (far left, bottom) and guitarist Dave Parsons, hailed from Hersham in northwest Surrey and took their name from some graffiti featuring their home village. They were authentic purveyors of Punk, gaining a cult following among skinheads. Their breakthrough year was 1978, when they released 'Angels with Dirty Faces' and 'If the Kids are United' – the latter was used at a Labour Party conference in 2005.

PUNK EVOLUTION

FASHION AND POETRY

In its initial stages Punk fashion was essentially anti-fashion. Punks raided charity shops – like hippies had before them – looking for old jeans, sweatshirts and T-shirts, which they then downgraded. Trousers were torn and tights were laddered to create a 'proletarian chic', with black the predominant colour. Padlocks and even razor blades were used as pendants, while safety pins had the dual purpose of holding clothes together and acting as jewellery. Short, cropped hair – as worn by this girl (above) with 'No Future' inked on her forehead – was at first the standard Punk hairstyle, before the elaborate Mohican became fashionable. Body piercing was another Punk trend. Studs and pins could end up in all sorts of places other than the traditional ear lobes – noses, eyebrows, lips, cheeks, even the tongue.

Punk infiltrated other areas of life and culture. In literature, the Punk presence was most famously embodied by the performance poet John Cooper Clarke (left), whose quick-fire, witty rhyming verses charted the ups and downs of working-class life. With his trademark shades and mop of wiry, back-combed hair, Clarke became as familiar to rock audiences as most of the bands, frequently performing as a warm-up act for the Sex Pistols, the Buzzcocks and Siouxsie and the Banshees.

HEAT WAVE – THE SUMMER OF 1976

SUMMER SCENES
For most people, the long hot weather was a welcome change from Britain's more variable summers. In towns and cities, parks filled up at lunchtime with office workers (bottom left) who unashamedly stripped off to soak up the sun. Even policemen sometimes succumbed to the heat (left) and welcomed the chance to take off their helmets and take a load off their feet. Tables appeared on pavements outside pubs and cafés. At sporting events, for once spectators were shading their heads from sun rather than rain. The tennis fans below were watching 20-year-old Björn Borg beating Ilie Nastase on a baking Centre Court at Wimbledon to win the first of his five consecutive men's singles titles.

The summer of 1976 burnt itself indelibly on the memories of all who experienced it. Many parts of England and Wales recorded zero rainfall during the second half of July and most of August, while temperatures soared into the 30s – and stayed there. Heathrow recorded 16 consecutive days at 32°C. Even in normally showery April there were places in Cornwall that stayed completely dry. Milton Abbas in Dorset and Teignmouth in south Devon shared the distinction of going a record 45 rainless days.

SCORCHED EARTH

As the unrelenting heat continued and the rainfall stayed away, the face of Britain began to dehydrate on a massive scale. Reservoirs shrank to a fraction of their usual size. The Pitsford Reservoir in Northamptonshire (above) – the water supply to more than 4 million people – became a dry and cracked lake bed, looking more like a water-starved East Africa than the East Midlands of England.

Even Wales ran short of water, with some reservoirs completely drying up, forcing the introduction of water rationing. Rivers were badly affected, too. In London the Thames shrank to little more than a trickle. Boats that would normally be bobbing on the water at Strand-on-the-Green near Chiswick in west London found themselves well and truly beached (far right). At nearby Kew Gardens, the total rainfall from the start of October 1975 to the end of

August 1976 was just half the normal level. Water suddenly became precious. Hosepipes and the watering of lawns were outlawed. Posters like this one (right) encouraged people to save water in any way they could, but most homes in 1976 did not have showers. People became used to taking shallow baths, then putting the water to another use when they had finished, such as pouring it onto their parched gardens or using it to flush the loo.

'... it was a very dry scenario ... There was no rain at all over most of England and Wales for several weeks ... Skies were almost cloudless.'

The Met Office

SAVE WATER

SHOWER WITH A FRIEND

HEAT AND DUST

For anyone who lived in Britain through the Seventies, one of the abiding memories of 1976 – and indeed the entire decade – was the long hot summer, which gave everyone a taste of the Costa del Sol without having to leave home. Long before the issue of 'global warming' was current, sun-lovers revelled in a sustained, guilt-free and it seemed never-ending spell of hot, dry, sunny weather such as they had rarely experienced in this country before – or would enjoy afterwards. The statisticians at the Met Office had a field day. They calculated that the drought (which ended in September) was the final phase of a sixteen-month period that was the driest since records began in 1727.

Of course, endless days of blue skies and desert-white suns might have been paradise for holiday-makers and ice-cream sellers, but it was wretched for farmers and many homeowners, especially those with houses built on clay soil, who faced insurance haggling as instances of subsidence increased with the dry weather. Britain's wild life suffered, too, not least from the drying up of rivers, which were reduced to muddy trickles. The most intense period of heat arrived on 23 June. For two solid weeks many places in the south enjoyed (or suffered, depending on the point of view) temperatures of 32°C or above. On 28 June Southampton recorded 35.6°C, the country's highest reading of the month.

Fire and drought

The combination of dryness and extraordinary heat led to the outbreak of a huge number of fires. Surrey firefighters were alerted to some 11,000 fires in five months. In Dorset a 30-foot wave of flame destroyed 250 acres of woodland near Ferndown. At a nearby hospital, more than 300 patients – some of them in wheelchairs and beds – and staff had to be evacuated in case the building was engulfed. Fortunately there were no casualties. But the flames also threatened a camp site and a military fuel depot. In the end a combination of 360 determined firefighters and soldiers, using a range of fire appliances – including two requisitioned milk tankers – got the fire under control. In the Lake District, the Haweswater reservoir shrank so low that the village of Mardale, not seen since it disappeared beneath the water when the reservoir was created back in the 1920s, reappeared like a ghost from its watery grave. Sightseers could see the old church tower, the walls of houses and dry-stone walls still enclosing what were once fields.

Towards the end of August, to coordinate efforts to combat the effects of the hot weather, the government appointed Denis Howell as 'Minister of Drought'. As television reports showed disappearing reservoirs, water restrictions were put in place and people were urged to 'think before you turn the tap on'. The *Blue Peter* programme advised placing a brick in toilet cisterns. There was a ban on using garden hosepipes and automatic car washes, as well as filling swimming pools and watering parks and sports fields. British Rail stopped washing their trains. People in Wales had their water supplies cut, and in Devon and Yorkshire standpipes had to be brought into use. The rains came back in September and gradually, over the following months, the reservoirs and rivers refilled and restrictions were eased. It was back to normal, but in some ways – pavement café tables, for example – the summer of 76 left its mark on the face of Britain.

STREET LIFE

The Falls Road area in Belfast (above), predominantly the home of working-class Catholics, was rife with tension throughout the Seventies. Small-scale street battles between nationalists – often teenagers and children, as here – and British soldiers and the RUC were part of everyday life. The Provisional IRA began 1976 by ending a ceasefire agreed the previous February with the British government. Thereafter, loyalist and republican paramilitaries were involved in regular violence and murder. In July, Christopher Ewart Biggs, the British Ambassador to the Republic of Ireland, was killed by a car bomb in Dublin.

Summer troubles

The long hot summer also witnessed – and might possibly have exacerbated – the usual sectarian strife in Northern Ireland, as well as racial tensions in London and elsewhere. In Northern Ireland, a rare outbreak of positive news occurred in August when two women, Mairead Corrigan and Betty Williams, started a peace movement. Within weeks they had organised a mass rally in Belfast where more than 10,000 Catholics and Protestants turned out to say enough is enough. The Peace People, as the movement was called, was born out of tragic events that occurred on 10 August, when Corrigan's sister, Anne Maguire, saw her three children run over by a car driven wildly by an IRA fugitive who had just been wounded by British soldiers. Corrigan, along with Betty Williams, a woman who had witnessed the tragedy, were galvanised to voice their anger on behalf of all women who had lost husbands and family, especially children, in the Troubles.

MURDER AND MAYHEM ON MAINLAND BRITAIN

The bombs and violence of Northern Ireland arrived on the mainland in the 1970s. Londoners in particular became wary of unattended packages. The attacks were indiscriminate, often claiming the lives of ordinary civilians. One such victim was the cancer expert Professor Gordon Hamilton-Fairley, who was killed in Holland Park on

22 October, 1975, when his dog accidentally set off a bomb intended for his neighbour, the Tory MP Sir Hugh Fraser. Even when the bombs did not maim or kill – such as the 12 small devices that exploded in London's West End on 29 January, 1976 – they created a climate of fear. London had got its first taste of the IRA bombing campaign on

8 March, 1973, when four large car bombs were planted around the city. Bomb-disposal experts defused two of them, but the others went off in Whitehall (below) and outside the Old Bailey. One man was killed and almost 200 people were injured. The following year, on 17 June, the IRA set off a 20lb-bomb in Westminster Hall at the

House of Commons (below right), which injured 11 people. Liberal MP David Steel saw the explosion: '... the whole hall was filled with dust. A few minutes later it was possible to see flames shooting up through the windows.' On 22 February, 1972, in retaliation for Bloody Sunday, the IRA detonated a bomb at the headquarters of the Parachute Regiment in Aldershot (right). Six civilians were killed – five female waitresses and a Catholic army chaplain.

Carnival violence

The August Bank Holiday carnival in Notting Hill had been a familiar and colourful fixture in London's summer calendar for a decade. In 1976 the crowds turned out as usual to enjoy the huge parade, but this year it turned ugly and violent. To many observers, the trouble was symptomatic of a rising tide of racial tensions which, perhaps inevitably, was fuelled by the failing economy. The trouble began on the Portobello Road when police tried to detain an alleged black pickpocket. Others went to help him, and before anyone knew it the situation had escalated: a running battle between police and black youths ensued, with the police improvising with dustbin lids for shields. Windows were smashed, a police van was set alight and gangs of white youths joined in the fracas.

The police tried to stem the violence by closing off roads and ordering pubs to close. In the end, more than 100 policemen were treated in hospital along with 60 carnival-goers. Nearly 70 people were arrested, but of these only 17 youths faced charges. Only two youths were eventually convicted of offences in a court case that cost £250,000, a record at the time. Afterwards, a mournful member of the carnival committee summed up his disappointment: 'This was supposed to be about fun and love – not violence.'

The National Front, Anti Nazi League and Rock Against Racism

The racial tensions that surfaced at the carnival were a recurring feature of the 1970s, with the far-right National Front (NF) movement often involved in violent clashes with anti-fascist groups, such as the Anti Nazi League (ANL). The National Front had formed in 1967 from other far-right movements, and in the early 1970s, with John Tyndall as leader, it gathered momentum. By mid-decade

OUT OF CONTROL
Carnival-goers watch nervously (top right) as the mood turns sour in Notting Hill, west London, in August 1976. The Notting Hill area had been home to Afro-Caribbeans since the 1940s. In 1958 it had seen serious racial violence, when some 300 white youths attacked the homes of black residents. The carnival was begun as a way to celebrate black culture in Britain. By 1976 it was in its tenth year and an estimated 150,000 people turned up to watch the parade and enjoy the party.

About 3,000 police officers had been deployed at the parade in case of trouble, but they were ill-prepared and poorly equipped. When violence broke out in Portobello Road, following a failed attempt to arrest a suspected pickpocket, the police were forced to beat a hasty retreat (bottom right). They grabbed anything that came to hand – dustbin lids, milk crates, bits of fencing – to defend themselves against a shower of bricks and bottles.

CARNIVAL CHAOS IN NOTTING HILL

it was beginning to make an electoral impact at a local level, attracting mostly blue-collar voters anxious about job competition from immigrants. The NF claimed to be a patriotic party and denied Nazi links, but its call for the mandatory repatriation of coloured Commonwealth immigrants caused outrage and retaliatory protest.

On 13 August, 1977, a year after the violence in Notting Hill, ugly scenes involving the National Front occurred during the 'battle of Lewisham' in south London. An NF march from New Cross to Lewisham was met by anti-fascist demonstrators, who pelted the marchers with smoke bombs, bricks, bottles and other objects. The police, who were escorting the marchers, were caught in the crossfire. By the end of the day more than a hundred people had been injured and more than 200 arrested.

The chief anti-NF protesters were the Anti Nazi League, founded in 1977 by members of the Socialist Workers' Party with the support of some trade unions. Its raison d'être was to fight the National Front, which it did with great commitment. Its main ally in this task was the influential Rock Against Racism (RAR), a loose, grassroots

BRANCHING OUT
Rock Against Racism was at the forefront of raising the consciousness of young people to the threat of the National Front. Their first big concert, at Victoria Park in Hackney, was held after an Anti Nazi League rally in Trafalgar Square on 30 April, 1977. Organisers expected 20,000 people to turn up, not the 80,000 who crammed into the park to watch the Clash (joined by Jimmy Pursey of Sham 69), Tom Robinson, X-Ray-Spex, Steel Pulse and Patrick Fitzgerald. The sound system left a lot to be desired, but it did not prevent a heaving mass of fans pogoing to songs such as the Clash's 'White Riot'. For those who wanted a better view of the stage, there were some good vantage points in the trees (right).

association of pop, rock and reggae musicians. Rock Against Racism came into being in 1977, partly in response to alleged racist and ultra-rightwing remarks by veteran rock guitarist Eric Clapton and David Bowie. On 30 April, 1978, the movement teamed up with the ANL to stage a one-day carnival in London that would prove an inspiration to those opposed to the NF. Heavy rain in the morning failed to dampen the spirits of the huge crowd who had come from Manchester, Sheffield, Glasgow and other parts of the country to gather in Trafalgar Square. From there they marched to Victoria Park in the East End – the NF's heartland – and in the afternoon, with the sun starting to appear, an array of performers headlined by the Clash and Tom Robinson entertained an audience that had grown to about 80,000. It was a spectacular success and, by the end of 1978, RAR had organised some 300 gigs in their fight against fascism. Many credit them with the decline of the National Front in the last part of the decade.

THE SILVER JUBILEE

In 1977 the whole country stopped to celebrate the Silver Jubilee of Queen Elizabeth II. Later commentators would reflect with nostalgia on the widespread display of innocent merrymaking. The first months of the year saw a modest recovery, or at least a stabilisation, in Britain's economy and perhaps a sense that the government was at last getting a grip fed into the mood of joyful optimism.

STREET SERVICE
On 7 June, 1977, Jubilee street parties were held all over Britain – there were an estimated 4,000 in London alone. In some cases people had been preparing for the party for months with raffles, cake stalls, coffee mornings and bring-and-buy events held to raise money. This one (right) was in Greatorex Street in London's East End, with tables set up, appropriately enough, outside the Queen's Head pub, which no longer exists. Jubilee Crescent in Gravesend in Kent drew the attention of the media, including BBC's *Nationwide*, by hosting two parties – rival affairs at either end of the street.

LONG LIVE THE QUEEN
In its innocence and joyful camaraderie, Queen Elizabeth's Silver Jubilee was like turning the clock back to 1952 itself. Union Jacks were everywhere – in flags waved by children, in house windows, in the bunting strung from roofs and lamposts that brightened up streets in preparation for a Jubilee party. Some towns put on parades – one was staged in Granada Television's long-running soap, *Coronation Street* – with floats and organised games for children. Jubilee souvenirs included the usual teaspoons, mugs, plates and tea caddies decorated with a youthful Queen Elizabeth, plus Union Jack hats – like the one worn by this little boy (left) – and flags bearing her portrait.

CELEBRATING OUT AND ABOUT
On Jubilee Day, 7 June, a beaming Queen
Elizabeth chats to some of the thousands of
people who lined the streets to watch her
Jubilee procession (top left). On the same
day she made a speech at the Guildhall in
which she declared: 'My Lord Mayor, when I
was twenty-one I pledged my life to the
service of our people and I asked for God's
help to make good that vow. Although that
vow was made in my salad days, when I was
green in judgement, I do not regret nor

retract one word of it.' Some of the
residents of the Aintree Estate in Fulham left
no doubt of their support and affections
(bottom left). The core celebrations ended
on 9 June with the Queen taking a boat trip
on the Thames, recalling the Tudor barge
trips taken by her namesake, Elizabeth I. On
the same day she formally opened the Silver
Jubilee Walkway and Jubilee Gardens on the
Southbank, then after a spectacular firework
display she returned to Buckingham Palace
in a procession of lit carriages.

JUBILEE YEAR TRIUMPH
It seemed nothing could go wrong in the
Jubilee summer. That year, Virginia Wade
even won the women's singles title at
Wimbledon. Here she is on 1 July, 1977,
raising the famous plate on centre court.
Her win was particularly appropriate, not
just because it was the Queen's Jubilee,
but because it was also the centenary of
the Wimbledon tennis tournament. Virginia
Wade remains the last Briton to lift a
singles trophy at the home of tennis.

Silver celebrations

Before the royal family became the stuff of tabloid headlines in the Eighties and
Nineties, it was an institution well respected by all apart from a few dyed-in-the-
wool republicans. The Queen commanded particular affection, and never was this
more evident than during the celebrations to mark her first 25 years on the throne.
On 6 February, the actual 25th anniversary of the Queen's accession, special
church services were held across the country. Over the next few months
preparations were made for the celebrations proper, which culminated in June.

The Queen was determined to visit as many of her subjects as possible, and
her grand tour of Britain and the Commonwealth countries began in May with a
trip to Glasgow. From there the royal entourage, greeted by huge crowds wherever
they went, moved on to England, Wales and Northern Ireland, where security was
intense. Later in the year the Queen travelled to Australia, New Zealand, Fiji,
West Indies, Canada and other countries. Everywhere she went she was greeted
with great warmth from flag-waving well-wishers.

On the night of 6 June, back at Windsor Castle, the Queen lit a bonfire that
ignited a chain of other fiery beacons across the country. On the following day,
St Paul's Cathedral became the focus of world attention as the Queen, dressed in
pink and driven in her golden state carriage, attended a thanksgiving service with
Prince Philip and the rest of her family. The rain could not dampen the spirits of
the thousands who had camped out overnight to gain good vantage points from
which to see the flotilla of carriages making its way from the Mall to the
cathedral, via Trafalgar Square and Fleet Street.

The service was attended by former prime ministers, from Harold Wilson
back to Harold Macmillan, and various world leaders including US President
Jimmy Carter. Later, the Queen and Prince Philip chatted with spectators and
received their cards and flowers. The procession then made its way down the Mall
back to Buckingham Palace, watched by crowds estimated at a million strong.
There were numerous balcony appearances, greeted with cheers and singing. The
events were televised and beamed abroad to some 500 million people. Meanwhile,
all around the country street parties were taking place. Neighbours who rarely
uttered more than a 'good morning' to each other found themselves sitting down
at long tables to eat together, either out on the street or in village halls and barns.

Wimbledon and cricket

The Silver Jubilee year held some golden sporting highlights. At Wimbledon,
Virginia Wade won the Ladies' Singles trophy, watched by the Queen at her first
attendance at the championships during her reign. Wade reached the final by

overcoming the American Chris Evert, a stalwart of the Championship, in the semi-finals in three sets. Her opponent in the final was Betty Stöve, a tall, hard-hitting Dutchwoman. A nervous Wade lost the first set 6-4. But urged on by the partisan crowd, she stormed back to win the next two sets 6-3, 6-1.

Another piece of summer sporting success was England's triumph against Australia in the cricket. Against an Australian team weakened by players defecting to Kerry Packer's World Series Cricket, a breakaway professional competition, England won the Ashes series 3-0, with two tests drawn. Strengthened in the batting by the return of the ever-dependable Geoff Boycott, England also unveiled a new talent in the third test at Trent Bridge, home of Nottinghamshire County Cricket Club. The 21-year-old Ian Botham took five Australian wickets in the first innings of his debut. Botham went on to become one of England's greatest all-rounders and a scourge of Australian teams, especially in 1981.

Back to reality

Below the surface of 1977's summer optimism and escapism there nevertheless bubbled the ugliness of racism and of strife in the workplace. A major focus of industrial trouble was the Grunwick Photo Processing Plant in Willesden in northwest London. The problems had started back in the summer of 1976, when some of the staff – mostly female Asians – had walked out of the plant in protest at poor pay and working conditions. When they subsequently joined the union APEX, the Grunwick owner, George Ward, sacked them all, since he did not want a unionised labour force. The dispute escalated, with the TUC calling for other unions to support the strikers.

By the spring of 1977 the tension at Grunwick had increased considerably. Picket lines were set up, and in May three Labour ministers, including Shirley Williams, joined the protesters. Then, during June and July, events took a turn for

WORKERS UNITED
The women workers sacked from their jobs at the Grunwick Photo Processing Plant were led by Jayaben Desai (right), who became treasurer of the strike committee. Desai was born in Gujarat in India and lived in Tanzania before moving to Britain in 1969. She started work at Grunwick in 1974. Dismayed by the poor working conditions and the management style, she led a walkout of staff on 20 August, 1976, after a dispute with the company over a demand to work overtime at short notice. The strike dragged on for two years, finally ending only on 14 July, 1978. Although the strikers had the sympathy of many, from fellow trade unionists to government ministers, none of the sacked workers was ever reinstated.

RUNNING RACIST BATTLES
A clash between National Front supporters and their anti-fascist opponents in Birmingham in August 1977. The National Front planned a series of deliberately provocative marches that August, staged predominantly in areas with significant numbers of immigrants. Anti-racist organisations, the Anti Nazi League and others among them, turned out to confront and oppose them. It fell to the police to keep the opposing sides apart. Serious violence in Birmingham prompted local councils to stop National Front marches on the grounds of public order and safety.

the worse when the pickets were reinforced by members of the Socialist Workers Party and other trade unions. These included a consignment of miners led by Arthur Scargill, then president of the Yorkshire NUM. The dispute reached a climax when up to 10,000 pickets, confronted by 3,700 police, tried to prevent the plant from operating. On 24 June clashes resulted in 52 arrests and injuries to seven policemen. Labour MPs, including a number of Cabinet members, were vocal in support of the strikers; but Jim Callaghan, concerned that Scargill would escalate the dispute, called a public inquiry. The strike dragged on until the summer of 1978 and all the while the antagonism, verging at times on violence, was a reminder that the country's underlying industrial ills had not gone away.

FLYING THE FLAG

The British airline industry in the Seventies received a massive psychological boost with the arrival of Concorde. The sight of the elegant supersonic airliner shimmering across the skies was a continual source of wonder and pride. Concorde was a joint development between BAC (the British Aircraft Corporation) and France's Aérospatiale. The plane had its first test flight in March 1969. This promotional photograph (right), with a line-up of stewardesses from different airlines, was taken in 1970 when hopes were still high that Concorde would be sold around the world. But by the time the first planes came into service – in January 1976 when regular flights began from London Heathrow to Bahrain – the oil crisis had changed attitudes as far as flying was concerned. Aeroplane capacity, rather than speed, was the primary concern and the Jumbo Jet was the plane of the moment. Another problem was noise. Flights to New York did not begin until November 1977, after a ban imposed on Concorde because of noise concerns was lifted. Passengers and the public back

at home loved the plane. Although space was at a premium, the service was first-class and with Concorde reducing the flying time to the USA by half, it soon became hugely popular with business travellers.

Freddie Laker's Skytrain (above) was a welcome innovation at the other end of the transatlantic market. Whereas Concorde catered for wealthy travellers to the USA, Freddie Laker made it possible for the rest of us to fly there. He originally started up his airline in 1966 but it was only in 1977 that he finally managed to pull all the required permissions together to launch his cheap, walk-on, transatlantic air service from London Gatwick to New York's JFK airport. The inaugural flight was on 26 September and the service was soon hailed as a great success that broke the mould for long-distance travel. But it lasted only until February 1982, when Laker Airways went bust. Various causes contributed to the bankruptcy, including over-expansion, but Laker's claim of aggressive unfair competition by the established airlines was given credence by a settlement out of court.

DISCONTENT
BUBBLES OVER

In the autumn of 1977, many people basked in the afterglow of the Jubilee celebrations, sharing a sense of cautious optimism about the economy. Denis Healey's August mini-budget was generally well received, the pound was gaining strength and share prices were on the up. The trauma of the IMF-imposed financial cuts was fading, the balance of payments was looking more rosy and annual inflation – which had risen to a frightening 25 per cent in the last weeks of 1975 – was now falling. So how did it all go so wrong for James Callaghan and the Labour government?

LOAD OF RUBBISH The so-called 'winter of discontent' of 1978–9 reminded everyone – all too visibly – of the fragile relationship between the unions and the Labour government. This temporary rubbish dump is in fact Leicester Square, at the time dubbed 'Fester Square'.

A MODEST RECOVERY

Although the Grunwick strike prevented any complacency that industrial antagonism was a thing of the past, it did seem possible that the government had turned a corner. Jim Callaghan gave off a sense of confidence and composure. Not only was he basking in the glow of a successful Jubilee, he had also forged an alliance with David Steel of the Liberal Party that helped him to live with his slender majority.

The catalyst for what became known as the Lib-Lab pact was a vote of no confidence in the government tabled by the Conservatives on 23 March, 1977. Callaghan approached Steel and a deal was struck. In return for supporting the government with their 13 MPs, the Liberals were offered the chance to consult with the government over policy-making. As Leader of the Opposition, Margaret Thatcher declared that Labour was 'more concerned to cling to office than it is to seek the verdict of the people'. In the event, the government saw off the Tory challenge by 322 votes to 298, and the Lib-Lab pact would hold for a year. Margaret Thatcher, meanwhile, was hedged in by former Heath loyalists and failing to make the impact that a new party leader might have hoped for.

Yet for all the positive economic news, there were sharp reminders of the chaos of recent years. The government's economic policy hinged on pay restraints, and by late 1977 it was insisting on a 10 per cent pay ceiling for public sector workers. On 14 November, firemen went on strike demanding a massive 30 per cent wage increase – three times the government's target figure.

SOLDIERS AND GODDESSES
The government responded to the firemen's strike in November 1977 by drafting in soldiers along with the army's ancient Green Goddess fire engines (below). The latter were in fact modified Bedford military trucks manufactured in the 1950s for use in the Auxiliary Fire Service. They were used as a back-up to the regular fire service in times of local or national crises, such as pumping out water during floods, or transporting water during droughts. Although the vehicles were officially mothballed in the late Sixties, the engines were maintained by the military in case of firemen's strikes. They not only saw use in 1977 but came out again 25 years later in the firemen's strike of 2002-3.

Troops to the pumps

As the firemen's strike began, their union claimed that more than 97 per cent of its members were refusing to answer calls. In response, the government drafted in some 10,000 troops to handle emergencies, even though the soldiers lacked proper training and equipment, relying on outdated 'Green Goddess' fire engines.

In the following weeks, the firemen's resolve was fully tested. When, for example, troops arrived to tackle a fire that had broken out at a hospital in Bow, East London, sympathetic firemen went to help and were instrumental in dousing the blaze. One of the firemen said afterwards: 'We couldn't let them die. For God's sake, it was a hospital, what else could we do but come and help?' On the other hand, a woman in Wallington in Surrey felt the full force of the strike. When a gas container exploded in her house, she fled to safety with her two sons, but then for 25 minutes had to watch the blaze devouring her home before troops arrived from Croydon – her local fire brigade would have taken just 3 minutes to reach her.

On 21 December the firemen tried to pressurise the government by persuading the TUC to vote for a public campaign against the 10 per cent ceiling. But the TUC general council voted against the firemen's proposal, the narrow margin of 20 votes to 17 clearly showing a division of opinion among the unions over the government's economic strategy. The firemen called off the strike in January 1978, accepting a 10 per cent rise but with guarantees of increases in the future.

STRIKING FOR MORE

On average, firemen worked a basic 48-hour week for an annual salary of about £3,700 a year. Their strike action received much sympathy from the public, from whom they received many donations during the run-up to Christmas 1977. These firemen, picketing outside Lambeth fire station, state their claim eloquently. One placard lists the range of problems they have to deal with – 'hazardous chemical incidents, road accidents, train crashes, sewers, floods etc' – and 'all for £46 per week'. Another placard states 'Remember Moorgate and Flixboro', referring to the Moorgate underground crash in February 1975 and the explosion at the chemical plant at Flixborough near Scunthorpe in June 1974 which claimed the lives of 28 people and seriously injured 36 more.

Election postponed

In early 1978 confidence in recovery was still reasonably high. But by spring the pound was coming under renewed pressure and the government had to face a Conservative Party that had spruced up its image by hiring the advertising agency Saatchi & Saatchi. It was the first public sign that the Tories were gearing up for a general election campaign that was expected as early as the autumn.

Labour's troubles increased when, in July, Callaghan announced that the new guideline for pay rises would be 5 per cent, starting on 1 August. Even many of his supporters believed that the figure was too low and therefore unworkable. Within a week the TUC had rejected the ceiling and demanded the reinstatement of free collective bargaining. Yet, at the same time, Labour was doing well in the polls, with some putting them ahead of the Tories. This led to widespread media speculation that Callaghan would call an autumn election. The party at large also seemed to expect – and want – an autumn election.

During the summer recess, Callaghan wavered. The Liberal Party MPs withdrew their support in July and he began to doubt whether he could muster the decisive Commons majority needed to avoid the political tightrope act required to stay in power. Finally, on 7 September, he announced that the election would be held in 1979. With the benefit of hindsight, many commentators see this as a fatal error and that Callaghan missed his best chance of defeating the Tories. Certainly, there was a general sense of deflation after the buzz surrounding the possibility of an autumn election. Callaghan himself now seemed unsure of his ground. He realised that Labour's current buoyancy could quickly disappear with any industrial unrest during the winter. In this he was proved right.

YOUNG CONSERVATIVE
The 16-year-old William Hague addressing the Conservative Party conference in Blackpool on 13 October, 1977. Even at such a precocious young age, he knew how to give his audience what they wanted. Claiming to speak for the young people of Britain, he said: 'They don't want to go to Callaghan's promised land, which must surely rank as the most abhorrent and miserable land that's ever been promised to the people of a nation state. But most of all they want to be free, free from the government – the government they think should get out of the way … and I trust that Mrs Thatcher's government will indeed get out of the way.' He was given a standing ovation and Thatcher declared she was 'thrilled' by the speech.

FORD STRIKE

The winter of discontent effectively got underway with the strike at Ford Motors in September 1978. At first the strike was unofficial, but Moss Evans, who had replaced Jack Jones as General Secretary of the TGWU earlier in 1978, backed the Ford workers and by October the full weight of the TGWU was behind them. Ford had a proud record in the UK, opening its first factory in Manchester in 1911, the first to be built outside America. By 1978 it had 57,000 UK employees, all of whom downed tools and came out on strike for an annual wage increase above the government's stated limit of 5 per cent. There was no division or disagreement among the workers and no picket lines were required. These Ford workers (right) took part in a march from Tower Hill to Westminster on 11 October. The workers knew the company had the money to increase their offer – hence the T-shirt logos – but were unwilling to do so because of the government's pay policy.

Trouble at Ford

Significant industrial problems surfaced in the autumn and were to accelerate into a crisis during the winter. First of all, workers at Ford Motors went on strike on 22 September in protest at a pay offer from Ford management set within the government's 5 per cent limit. Ford had made enough profits the previous year to have offered more money, but the company did not wish to incur the government's threatened sanctions for breaching the pay limit.

Meanwhile, on 2 October, the Labour Party conference passed a motion proposing that the government should not interfere with wage negotiations – a vote that Jim Callaghan reluctantly accepted. In late November, Ford offered its workers a pay rise of 17 per cent, which they accepted. But in doing so the company had set a precedent that Callaghan feared would lead to exaggerated pay claims and an upturn in inflation.

The government responded to Ford's settlement by imposing sanctions on the company – along with more than 200 other companies that had breached the official 5 per cent pay-claim guideline. This in turn elicited a furious response from the CBI and a protest by the Conservatives. On 13 December, the Conservative Opposition tabled a motion in the Commons against the sanctions and Callaghan lost the vote. The next day, he called for a vote of confidence in the government, which Labour won by just ten votes. But Callaghan knew that, with the sanctions effectively dead in the water, there was no mechanism to prevent wage claims soaring over the 5 per cent limit.

ESCAPING THE GLOOM

Many people were content to flee the grim headlines of industrial unrest and economic uncertainty by retreating into the alternative worlds provided by television and cinema. There was a vogue for science-fiction, with blockbuster films such as *Star Wars* and *Superman*, and the cult radio hit, the *Hitchhiker's Guide to the Galaxy*. Others escaped into the drama and intrigue of new soaps such as *Dallas*, centred around the flamboyant Ewing family; *Grange Hill*, a school saga set in a north London comprehensive; and *Minder*, with Dennis Waterman playing an amiable bodyguard to George Cole's Arthur Daley, a nattily dressed, wily wheeler-dealer.

Another programme that started in the late 1970s and went on to great success was *Top Gear*. Although it would later be associated with the irrepressible Jeremy Clarkson, it began life in 1977 in more restrained style with Angela Rippon and Noel Edmonds among the first presenters. It had a 30-minute slot and focused on the latest cars and motoring issues. For the more artistically and culturally inclined there was Melvyn Bragg's *South Bank Show*, which got underway on 14 January, 1978. In the first programme it showcased Germaine Greer, Gerald Scarfe and Paul McCartney. Also in 1978 Dennis Potter's *Pennies from Heaven* brought plaudits to its author and fame to actor Bob Hoskins, who starred in what became a trademark Potter mixture of reality and fantasy, with characters breaking into mimed renditions of 1930s songs.

TELEVISION TREATS

The Seventies was a golden age of TV comedy. The nation's best-loved comedy duo was Morecambe and Wise, who had begun working together back in 1941. By the mid-Seventies, their show was a weekly highlight for millions, with the power to attract guest stars of the calibre of Yehudi Menuhin, Rudolf Nureyev, Sir Laurence Olivier and the conductor André Previn. Eric and Ernie switched from BBC to ITV in 1978 and are pictured here (bottom right) advertising their new employers' TV guide. Their final show for the BBC at Christmas 1977 drew more than 28 million viewers – pretty much half the entire population. It featured, among others, Elton John (or 'Elephant John' as Eric called him), the cast of *Dad's Army* and Angela Rippon, who reprised the high-kicking dance routine that had gone down so well with viewers the year before.

One of the most original new comedy shows of the decade was *The Goodies* (far right) – from top to bottom Graeme Garden, Tim Brooke-Taylor and Bill Oddie. The trio lit up many a gloomy evening with their particular brand of breezy, witty and surreal sketches. They also had a hit song with 'Funky Gibbon'. The three had met at Cambridge where they performed in the University Footlights revue, before carving out careers on TV and radio.

Right at the end of the decade, ITV scored a huge hit with the comedy-drama *Minder*, starring Denis Waterman and George Cole (top right), first aired in October 1979. The show revolved around Arthur Daley (Cole), a dodgy, cigar-smoking, wheeler-dealer businessman, and his bodyguard, or 'minder', ex-boxer Terry McCann (Waterman).

In contrast, the lovely Delia Smith (left) from Woking in Surrey got her television break in 1973, when she first started teaching the nation how to cook. Her first series *Family Fare* ran for two years and established her as an engaging presenter and reliable guide to the mysteries of cooking. Her books also sold well through the decade, from her very first offering, *How to Cheat at Cooking* (1971), to her *Book of Cakes* (1977) and her classic three-volume *Cookery Course* (1978–80).

LOOKING ON THE BRIGHT SIDE

Sci-fi highs

From daybreak in Leicester Square on a cold 27 December, 1977, people queued to snap up tickets for *Star Wars*. The film had already blazed a box-office trail in the USA and was about to have its UK premier. Starring the virtually unknown Harrison Ford and Sir Alec Guinness, a veteran stalwart of British film and theatre, *Star Wars* was essentially a futuristic fairy tale drawing on proven Hollywood formats set alight by state-of-the-art special effects, some of which had been created in the Elstree Studios in London. The *Guardian*'s film reviewer Derek Malcolm commented: 'There is a space-age Western saloon, there's swashbuckling with laser beams, there's slapstick which reminds one of Laurel and Hardy and sentiment that reeks of *The Wizard of Oz*.' The British public loved it. In later years *Star Wars* spawned sequels and prequels to become the biggest movie series of all time.

In the following year, the sci-fi cinema extravaganza continued with *Superman*, based on the 1938 comic book creation. A stellar cast included Christopher Reeve as the eponymous hero doing battle with the evil Lex Luthor (played by Gene Hackman), while holding down a job at *The Daily Planet* in Metropolis in the guise of his alter ego, Clark Kent. Marlon Brando had a 15-minute cameo as Superman's father, a part that reputedly cost the film-makers $4 million.

For those who preferred a more British brand of sci-fi there was the hilariously quirky *Hitchhiker's Guide to the Galaxy*, written by Douglas Adams, which began as a BBC radio comedy in March 1978. It charted the adventures of Arthur Dent and his alien friend Ford Prefect as they travelled around space, starting with their escape from planet Earth just seconds before its demolition to make room for a new space superhighway. One of the most popular characters was the depressed robot, Marvin. The series was so successful it was repeated in the same year and went on to give birth to five bestselling books, a TV series and, eventually, a film.

LARGER THAN LIFE
Two colourful Seventies imports from the USA that would prove hugely popular. The three new stars of *Star Wars* were (top, from left to right) Mark Hamill as Luke Skywalker, Carrie Fisher as Princess Leia and Harrison Ford as Han Solo. *Dallas*, an everyday tale of Texan oil tycoons, first reached Britain's television screens in 1978. Before long, its audience was hooked and it ran for 13 years. The Ewing family were not always as happy as they appear in this promotional photo. From left to right, they are: back row, Patrick Duffy as Bobby and Larry Hagman as J R (John Ross) Ewing Jr; middle row, Victoria Principal as Pamela, Barbara Bel Geddes as Miss Ellie and Linda Gray as Sue Ellen; and front row, Charlene Tilton as Lucy and Jim Davis (1909–81) as John Ross 'Jock' Ewing.

Who watched JR?

Back down to earth, more or less, 1978 saw the start of one of TV's longest-running soap dramas – *Dallas*, an everyday tale of oil, power, sex and intrigue. For viewers in their terraced houses, used to drizzly rain and penny-pinching, it was the perfect escapist antidote and people lapped up their weekly dose of the fabulously rich Ewing family on their palatial Southfork ranch in sun-drenched Texas. The anti-hero of the series was J R Ewing, played by Larry Hagman, a machiavellian oil baron driving his wife, Sue Ellen, to drink. Balancing the wonderfully wicked character of J R was younger brother Bobby, whose marriage to Pamela from the Barnes family – hated by J R – added to the friction.

Football crazy

For some there was the weekly pilgrimage to the match to look forward to every Saturday. The BBC's *Match of the Day* enjoyed a golden decade, with viewing figures reaching as high as 12 million on a Saturday night.

Following the demise of Sir Alf Ramsey, it was a dismal decade for England's football fans. The England team repeated the embarrassment of 1974 by failing to qualify for the 1978 World Cup. For good measure they also missed out on the 1972 and 1976 European cups. Scottish fans fared far better. Scotland, with star strikers Archie Gemmell and Kennie Dalglish, followed up their good performance in the 1974 World Cup by qualifying for the 1978 World Cup in Mexico. Their fans also had the great delight of seeing the team beat England at Wembley in June 1977 to win the British Home Championship for the second year in succession.

To the enormous frustration of the England fans, the managers who succeeded Ramsey – Joe Mercer, Don Revie and Ron Greenwood – seemed to ignore, or include only occasionally, flair players such as Rodney Marsh, Peter Osgood, Stan Bowles, Tony Currie, Charlie George, Alan Hudson and Frank Worthington. These attacking players delighted the terraces week in, week out, always ready to exhibit – their critics might say over-indulge – their ball skills.

At club level, England were extraodinarily successful on the European stage, with English clubs winning eight European titles during the decade. The dominant team was Liverpool

STAR PLAYER
Liverpool were the in-form side in the Seventies and Kevin Keegan (right) was their leading light. With trademark permed hair and a broad smile, he played for Liverpool from 1971 to 1977, helping them to three League Championships and a European Cup win in 1977. In 1978 and 1979 he was given the ultimate accolade in European football, being voted player of the year for two years in succession.

under manager Bob Paisley. On a balmy Wednesday night in Rome on 25 May, 1977, the Reds beat German champions Borussia Mönchengladbach 3-1. It was a fitting farewell to Keegan, who left the club and the country at the end of that season to join Hamburg SV. The following May the scousers took the European Cup again, with a 1-0 victory over the Belgian club Brugge KV.

If the dominant club manager in the mid to late Seventies was Liverpool's Bob Paisley, his main rival – and certainly his superior in attracting headlines and notoriety – was the inimitable Brian Clough. Having enjoyed success with Derby County at the start of the decade, Clough joined Second Division Nottingham Forest in January 1975. It was the start of an amazing footballing fairy tale.

In the 1976–7 season, with the help of his old assistant Peter Taylor, Clough guided Forest to promotion to Division One. Then in 1978 Forest went on to win the League Championship for the first time in the club's history, also adding the League Cup to its silverware. And still the momentum continued. In February 1979 Clough signed Trevor Francis, Birmingham City's highly rated striker, in Britain's first £1 million football transfer. Francis repaid that faith in spades in the 1979 European Cup final against Swedish team Malmö FF, when his diving header earned Nottingham Forest a 1-0 victory and the trophy.

SWEDISH SENSATION
One of the biggest stars of sport in 1970s Britain was the tennis player Bjorn Borg. In 1976, aged just 20, he won the first of his Wimbledon championship titles. He went on to win the men's singles tournament in five consecutive years, from 1976 to 1980, a record that stood until 2009 when Roger Federer won a sixth consecutive title. Even before his first victory at Wimbledon, Borg had won the hearts of countless – mainly female – fans. Here he is surrounded by young autograph hunters during a pre-Wimbledon reception at the Hurlingham Club on 23 June, 1974.

SPORTING HIGHLIGHTS

For most of the decade, Scotland were the only British team to qualify for football's big international tournaments, but Liverpool and Nottingham Forest salvaged some pride for English football by winning the European Cup club championship. England's cricketers lost more than they won, although they did reach the one-day world cup final in 1979, losing to the West Indies. In rugby, Wales dominated the Five Nations' Championship throughout the decade. They also provided the spine of the British Lions team that beat the All Blacks for the first time in 1971.

NATIONAL FAVOURITE
The star of the track in the 1970s was Red Rum, winner of the Grand National a record three times – in 1973, 1974 and 1977. Here he is, ridden by jockey Tommy Stack, coming home for the third of those victories at Aintree on 2 April, 1977.

THE LIONS ROAR
In a rare international success for British teams in the Seventies, the British Lions scored an historic victory against the All Blacks in the 1971 test series in New Zealand, winning the series by two tests to one, with one match drawn. The Lions fielded the likes of Willie John McBride, the Irish lock; Barry John, the great Welsh fly half; J P R Williams, the fearless Welsh fullback; and, at scrum half, the legendary Gareth Edwards, here (bottom left) being tackled by New Zealand's Alan McNaughton. With the series tied after two matches, the crunch came in the third test at Wellington, when, thanks to tries by Barry John and Gerald Davies, the Lions won 13-3. A 14-14 draw in the final test ensured that the honours went to the tourists. Three years later the Lions, led by McBride, completed an unbeaten tour of South Africa.

EUROPEAN TRIUMPHS

In Rome on 25 May, 1977, goals from Terry McDermott, Tommy Smith and Phil Neal saw Liverpool beat Borussia Mönchengladbach to take the European Cup for the first time to the delight of their fans (below). They were only the third British team to lift the trophy since the tournament began in 1956, following Celtic (1967 champions) and Manchester United (1968). The banner in the centre refers to Joey Jones and his part in the defeat of French team St-Etienne and Swiss champions Zürich in earlier rounds.

Liverpool won both the League and the European trophy again the following year, but then a most unexpected team took over their crown. Brian Clough (left) had steered Nottingham Forest into the First Division in the 1976–7 season, then to the League Championship the following year. This qualified them to represent England in the European Cup, which they duly lifted in 1979.

THE LAST WORD

The test match at Lords between England and Australia in 1975 ended in a draw, but the proceedings were noticeably enlivened by the appearance of a streaker, who vaulted over the stumps (right), giving rise to ribald headlines in the newspapers the next day. Australia won the four-match series 1-0, with three tests drawn.

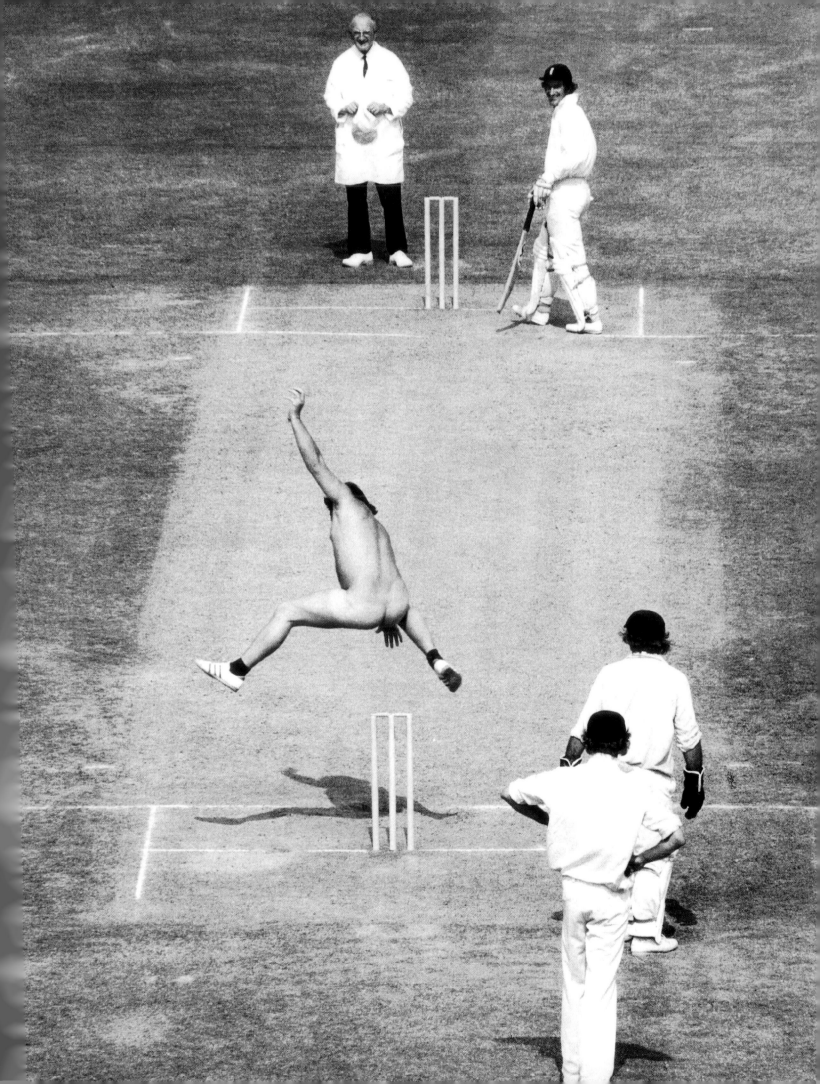

CRISIS? WHAT CRISIS?

In early January 1979, with politicians and the public wondering when the imminent general election would be held, Britain was plunged back into industrial chaos. Lorry drivers went out on strike – at first unofficially, then endorsed by the TGWU and the United Road Transport Union – demanding a 25 per cent pay rise. As drivers picketed oil refineries and thousands of workers were temporarily laid off, Britain looked as if it might literally grind to a halt. In the same month, James Callaghan flew off to the Caribbean island of Guadeloupe for a summit meeting with the leaders of the USA, Germany and France. It was unfortunate for him that the meeting was held in one of the world's prime holiday spots.

When Callaghan returned to Heathrow on 10 January, looking tanned and relaxed, he was met by a horde of reporters asking questions about the country's industrial crisis. He made it clear he would not be declaring a state of emergency and, when asked by a *Sun* reporter if he had been right to fly off from the country at this time, 'Sunny Jim' gave a reply that ended with the words: 'I promise if you look at it from the outside, I don't think other people in the world would share the view that there is mounting chaos.'

The next day, the *Sun* ran with the front-page headline 'Crisis? What Crisis?'. It was a crude summary of Callaghan's remarks – it was not even original, it was picked up from the title of a Supertramp album of 1975 – but it struck a chord with the public. It highlighted what seemed to be a yawning discrepancy between

OFF THE RAILS
The very infrastructure of the country seemed under threat during the Winter of Discontent. Rubbish piled up in the streets, and instead of busy trains there were empty platforms in the stations. Tracks into the major railway hubs were completely deserted. This is the scene of inactivity outside Waterloo on 17 January, 1979 (right). Some strikes took place without official union support, but a huge range of workers were involved in the stoppages, from journalists, pilots, civil servants and printers to cleaners, dinner ladies and traffic wardens. In total, some 30 million working days were lost through industrial action in 1979, compared to about 10 million in 1978.

NURSING ENCOURAGEMENT
Nurses outside St Andrew's Hospital in Bow, East London, encourage motorists to show support for their industrial action by tooting their horns. The nurses were members of NUPE (the National Union of Public Employees) and were taking part in a four-hour strike on 7 February, 1979. A couple of weeks earlier, on 22 January, 1979, public sector workers staged a day of action that saw the biggest mass rally in London since 1971, when some 140,000 had marched in protest against the Conservative government's Industrial Relations Act. David Basnett, General Secretary of the GMWU (General and Municipal Workers Union) described the demonstrators as those who 'literally care for us from the cradle to the grave'.

'It's quite obvious Mr Callaghan is out of touch with the deteriorating situation in Britain … to come back and suggest it all looks parochial is frankly patronising.'

Michael Heseltine, Shadow Industry Secretary and Conservative MP

the Prime Minister's perception of the situation and the chaos that appeared to be unfolding all around. Callaghan's lack of urgency played into the hands of Conservative MPs, who were now quick to call for a general election. The 'Winter of Discontent' had begun.

The Winter of Discontent

From mid January onwards events accelerated. Keenly aware that those in the private sector were asking for and being awarded significantly higher pay rises than the government's target figure of 5 per cent, a number of public sector workers began to test the government's resolve. Train drivers started a series of 24-hour strikes, while nurses put in a claim for a 25 per cent rise. The unions called for a reduction to a 35-hour working week with a minimum wage of £60.

On 22 January, 1979, the country was brought to a standstill by a day of action by public sector workers in support of more pay. More than a million workers went on strike in what was the biggest action of its kind since the General Strike of 1926. Tens of thousands marched through the streets of London, Edinburgh, Cardiff and Belfast. Hospitals had to make do without porters, cleaners and cooks. Even ambulance drivers joined in the strike, although some were prepared to answer emergency calls. Where they were not prepared to do so, the army was on stand-by. Airports were affected as manual staff did not turn up for work. Deprived of caterers, caretakers and lollipop ladies, hundreds of schools had to close. It all added up to a sense of a country winding down.

Over the next few weeks the strikes carried on, and still Callaghan resisted calling a state of emergency – despite, or perhaps because of, Margaret Thatcher's insistence that he should do so. Rubbish continued to accumulate, and local authorities had to make use of public spaces to store hundreds of bags of rotting refuse. London's Leicester Square became a refuge for rubbish bags and a haven for rats. But for many, the most shocking action was by gravediggers in Liverpool and Tameside, where they refused to bury the dead. Inevitably, the strikes turned the narrow poll lead Labour had gained in 1978 into a Conservative one.

All political parties sensed that a general election was nigh. The forcing point came on 1 March when the people of Scotland and Wales voted in a referendum on the issue of devolution. The Welsh voted against, while Scottish voters were in favour, but not sufficiently so to surpass the threshold of 40 per cent of the overall electorate as laid down by Parliament. The Scottish National Party, disenchanted by the lack of progress on devolution, withdrew their support from Labour. The Conservatives scented blood. Buoyed up by victory in two by-elections showing

continued on page 148

ZERO SHELF LIFE
With the lorry drivers on strike in January 1979, supplies of food failed to reach the shops and the shelves emptied. Here, shoppers size up what little is left in the meat section of a supermarket in Surrey. Essentials such as milk (costing 11p a pint) and bread (about 28p a large loaf) were the first food items to be snapped up. The situation was made worse by the Siberian weather conditions that descended on Britain that January and lasted into February, with snow at times making transport on road and rail impossible. Shoppers also had to cope with rising prices and, for many, the loss of paid employment: more than a million workers lost their jobs for a time because of strike action.

ISN'T
G.

BETTER OFF WITH THE CONSERVATIVES.

THE ART OF PERSUASION

With the professional help of the advertising agency Saatchi & Saatchi, the Conservative Party ran a clever and concerted campaign attacking the Labour government's record. They came up with the idea of focusing on an area that should have been Labour's strength – employment. Although jobs were easy to come by for most of the 1970s, unemployment started to rise as the decade went on and then shot up quite sharply in the Winter of Discontent. When Mrs Thatcher first saw the initial design for the poster (left), she objected at first that the immediate impact was the word 'Labour'. But she was then persuaded that the negative message would come across. In the event, only 20 posters were distributed, but such was their impact – magnified by the public objections of Labour Party supporters – that the media widely reproduced the image. What the unsuspecting public did not realise was that the queue of supposedly jobless workers were actually a group of Young Conservatives from South Hendon. Denis Healey declared the poster a fake, but this only added fuel to the blaze of publicity, which eventually made the poster one of the most iconic of the late 20th century.

significant swings in their favour – admittedly, more from the Liberals than from Labour – they tabled a vote of no confidence in the government for 28 March.

The vote in the House of Commons was tense – both sides knew it would be close. Labour had a set-back when one of their MPs, Sir Alfred Broughton, failed to attend because of illness. It turned out to be crucial: the government lost the motion by one vote – 311 to 310. The result was greeted by wild cheers from the Tories and defiant singing of 'The Red Flag' by the Labour faithful. Callaghan became the first Prime Minister to be compelled to hold a general election because of a Commons vote since Ramsay MacDonald in 1924. But he remained unbowed, declaring confidently that 'we shall take our case to the country'.

Election underway

The 1979 general election campaign began with a tragedy. On 30 March, Airey Neave, the Shadow Northern Ireland Secretary and a close friend and adviser of Margaret Thatcher, was killed by an IRA car bomb in Westminster. For a day, the rivals for Number 10 were united as they condemned the murder.

The three main parties spent the next five weeks wooing the voters. James Callaghan and the rest of the government tried to point out that they were on the right track – that inflation had been coming down and that the economy could only be improved by cooperation between management and workers. Their priorities included controlling inflation and prices; creating employment; and a pledge to strengthen world peace and defeat world poverty.

Mrs Thatcher had a completely new and different agenda. She pledged that a Conservative government would curb union power and cut public expenditure and income tax. She also played the patriotic card: '… there has been a feeling of helplessness, that we are a once-great nation that has somehow fallen behind and that it is too late now to turn things round. I don't accept that. I believe we not only can, we must.'

David Steel and the Liberals painted a picture of the two main parties engaged in 'confrontation politics' and stressed how their pact with Labour had made a difference. Steel maintained that effective government would rely not so much on 'which big dinosaur Party returns with the largest number of parliamentary seats than upon the size of the Liberal wedge in the House of Commons'.

INTO A NEW ERA

On 3 May, 1979, the country finally went to the polls. The Conservatives won by an overall majority of 43 seats. Some prominent MPs failed to regain their seats, including Shirley Williams (who would re-emerge in the SDP Party in the early 1980s) and the Liberal deputy leader John Pardoe. On the steps of 10 Downing Street, Margaret Thatcher – Britain's first woman Prime Minister – set out her vision of the future with the following words, a quote that she mistakenly attributed to St Francis of Assisi: 'Where there is discord, may we bring harmony. Where there is error, may we bring truth. Where there is doubt, may we bring faith. And where there is despair, may we bring hope.'

THE NEW PRIME MINISTER
A jubilant Margaret Thatcher, with her husband Denis by her side, greets the crowds in the first flush of her election victory. Denis would be a source of unwavering support to her during her time in office, but from the steps of Number 10 she paid a fulsome tribute to another man as the greatest male influence on her life and career – her father, Alfred Roberts.

'One small step for Margaret Thatcher, one giant stride for womankind.'

The Guardian, 4 May, 1979

NEW MAN IN CHARGE OF MONEY
Thatcher's first Cabinet was the least 'Thatcherite' of her entire premiership. It was packed full of left-of-centre Conservatives – Heathite MPs. One exception was her new Chancellor, Geoffrey Howe (above), who was an early and committed believer in the right-wing economic policies that would soon be known by all as 'monetarist'.

And so a new era began for Britain. It was the start of 11 years of Mrs Thatcher as Prime Minister and 17 years of continuous Conservative rule. During this time, Thatcher became one of the most dominant politicians of the 20th century, an ideologue who revelled in the day-to-day business of government, a conviction politician who could bludgeon opponents – and sometimes colleagues – into submission. She would also become a major figure on the world stage, a close friend and ally of US President Ronald Reagan and a Cold War warrior dubbed the 'Iron Lady' by a Moscow newspaper. Many would fail to recognise her opening sentiments in the actions that would follow, seeing her premiership as one of the most divisive in history. For others she would become a hero.

But in 1979 all this was still to come. For the moment, Thatcher had to appoint a Cabinet and get down to coping with the country's immediate problems. Many of the key posts went to former Heathites – those Thatcher would later dub 'wets' for their lack of zeal for her right-wing economic policy. Willie Whitelaw, for example, became Home Secretary, and despite his Heathite credentials proved a loyal colleague to Thatcher, prompting her to utter the immortal line, 'Every prime minister needs a Willie'. Lord Carrington was made Foreign Secretary, and Francis Pym headed the ministry of defence. The crucial post of Chancellor went to Sir Geoffrey Howe, who for many years remained a Thatcher loyalist.

One of Thatcher's previous, and dubious, claims to fame as Education Secretary had been to abolish free milk in state primary schools in the early 1970s. Now, ironically, within three weeks of her taking office, one of the first changes the country witnessed was a sharp increase in the price of milk by 10 per cent to 15p a pint – three times what it had cost in 1974. Bread, gas and electricity also went up, as did petrol by 6p a gallon.

Then, on 14 June, Geoffrey's Howe's first budget set out a financial agenda that would use monetary policy and interest rates to tackle inflation and marked a shift from direct to indirect taxation. VAT on most goods was almost doubled from 8 per cent to 15 per cent, while income tax was cut from 33 per cent to 30 per cent. He announced public spending cuts, stating that 'we cannot go on avoiding difficult choices'. But to everyone except the Tories, it seemed he was increasing tax on the poor in order to give more to the rich.

High-profile court case

While the country was absorbing the reality of the new government and the rise in basic prices, there were many other distractions in the news that summer of 1979. First and foremost, there was the drama of the Jeremy Thorpe court case which lasted 31 days, playing out like a soap opera to rival *Coronation Street*. The former Liberal leader and three other men were charged with conspiracy to murder the former male model Norman Scott. The Old Bailey jury reached a verdict of not guilty for all the defendants. Although he was found innocent, the

OLD PROBLEMS, NEW RESPONSE
When Mrs Thatcher brought the Conservatives to power in May 1979, industrial unrest did not go away. She faced the same problems with the unions as Jim Callaghan had faced – and before him Harold Wilson and Edward Heath – but she chose to meet them in a more confrontational style. In December 1979, teachers marched in London (above) to protest against education cuts proposed by ILEA (the Inner London Education Authority) as a result of cuts in funding from central government. Their posters portray the new Prime Minister as a 'mad axewoman'.

LIBERAL RELIEF
On 22 June, 1979, after a court case lasting a month, the former Liberal Party leader Jeremy Thorpe (right) and three other men were cleared of the charge of conspiring to murder Norman Scott (left). Responding to the not-guilty verdict after the trial, Thorpe said: 'I have always maintained that I was innocent of the charges brought against me and the verdict of the jury, after a prolonged and careful investigation by them, I regard as totally fair and a complete vindication.' The case attracted negative comments in the media about homosexuality, which angered supporters of the gay rights movement, some of whom are demonstrating here as Mr Thorpe arrives at the Old Bailey.

case had already ruined Thorpe's political career. He stood in the election in May, but was voted out of his north Devon constituency after 20 years as its MP.

New records

Meanwhile, in athletics a champion middle-distance runner emerged. On 17 July, in Oslo, Sebastian Coe broke the world record for the mile, completing the race in 3 minutes, 48.95 seconds to shave 0.4 seconds from John Walker's previous record, which had stood for four years. Coe remained unbeaten in all distances throughout the year, also breaking world records in the 800 and 1,500 metres.

If Thorpe and Coe dominated the front and the back pages in the early summer, August brought a story that the media could not resist: it was announced that Brighton would become the first major seaside resort in the country to have an official nudist beach. The campaign for nudism had been driven forward by local councillor Eileen Jakes, who apparently brought her colleagues around to her way of thinking by showing them photographs of herself bathing topless in Ibiza.

Tragedies on water

On 14 August, as the annual Fastnet sailing race reached the southern coast of Ireland, a freak storm hit. Distress calls were sent out by many of the 300-plus yachts taking part as winds of gale force strength drove the sea into mountainous waves. Royal Navy helicopters and rescue boats from Ireland, Britain and even Holland and France tried to haul the competitors to safety, but dozens of yachts were destroyed and 15 people lost their lives.

There was more grim news to come from Ireland. On 27 August, Lord Louis Mountbatten, the Queen's cousin, was killed by an IRA bomb planted on his boat in County Sligo. Mountbatten had been spending his usual summer holiday there at Classiebawn Castle and was taking the boat out from the fishing village of Mullaghmore when the bomb went off. One of Mountbatten's twin grandsons and

HELICOPTER HELP
The Fastnet yacht race began on a tranquil, sunny day on 11 August, 1979. Competitors set off from the Isle of Wight and headed across the Irish Sea to round the Fastnet Rock off the coast of west Cork, before returning to Plymouth. But a ferocious storm hit the yachts on 14 August. The rescue services were scrambled and Royal Navy helicopters managed to rescue some yacht crews by winching them to safety (above). Despite their efforts, 15 people lost their lives in the mountainous seas. One of the competitors who managed to return home unscathed was Edward Heath, who commented: 'It's an experience that I do not think anybody would want to go through again willingly.'

a local boy were also killed. A few hours later, 18 British soldiers were killed at Warrenpoint in South Down, the greatest number to die in a single incident in Northern Ireland. The atrocities inspired revenge killings as Loyalist paramilitaries targeted Catholic civilians. The decade was ending with the Troubles in full spate.

The Thunderer and spooks

One optimistic sign that industrial wrangles could be resolved by patient negotiation came with the reappearance of *The Times* after a year-long dispute over manning levels and the use of new technology. 'The Thunderer' had been printed continuously from 1788 until November 1978. Eventually, the Canadian owners, the Thomson Organisation, managed to negotiate a deal with the unions, and on 13 November, 1979, the newspaper returned – with a promise to include three extra obituary supplements to cover the backlog of deaths.

One of the first big stories that *The Times* was able to cover was the news, announced by Margaret Thatcher on 16 November, that Sir Anthony Blunt, the Queen's adviser on art, was the 'fourth man' in the Cambridge spy ring (the others were Guy Burgess, Donald Maclean and Harold 'Kim' Philby). The authorities had actually accused Blunt of treason in 1964, but had granted him immunity in return for his confession and future cooperation. With an imminent new book,

The Climate of Treason by Andrew Boyle, set to reveal Blunt's role, the government decided to bring it out into the open. Blunt was stripped of his knighthood and died three years later, his reputation in tatters.

The year closed with a significant pointer to future Conservative policy. On 20 December the government announced in its Housing Bill that council tenants would be given the right to buy – a measure that Michael Heseltine, Secretary of State for the Environment, declared to be 'one of the most important social revolutions of this century'. Labour accused the government of selling off national assets and warned that the poorest would suffer, but the Tories maintained that a larger property-owning public would be more socially responsible.

Indeed, the need for social responsibility – and hard work – was spelled out by Mrs Thatcher in an article in the *News of the World* on 30 December. It was, in effect, not only her new-year but her new-decade message. It signalled the end of the Seventies and rang out a personal note of optimism for the coming decade: 'Everyone can do something to help our country to recover. So as you raise a glass to the Eighties tomorrow night, drink with me to the awakening of Britain. Our enjoyment of the years ahead depends on our ability and willingness to work for it. If it is to be a "Dynamic Decade" for us all, these will be difficult and dangerous years. But we are drinking to a country with a future. Our future.'

LAID TO REST
The funeral procession of Lord Louis Mountbatten, assassinated by the IRA in County Sligo on 27 August, 1979. The coffin, draped in a Union Jack, was carried through the streets of London on a naval gun carriage on 5 September, 1979. On top of the coffin lie the admiral's regalia – the sword of honour, gold stick and cocked hat. The funeral cortege, which comprised members of Britain's armed forces along with delegations from India, Burma, the USA, France and Canada, made its way to Westminster Abbey. In traditional manner, the procession was led by Dolly, Lord Mountbatten's horse, with his master's boots reversed in the stirrups.

AND FINALLY ... PYTHONS IN THE DESERT

The Monty Python team photographed on location in Tunisia in 1978 while filming *Monty Python's Life of Brian*. From left to right: John Cleese, Terry Gilliam, Terry Jones, Graham Chapman, Michael Palin and Eric Idle. Cleese holds a perch with a stuffed parrot as a reminder of the famous 'dead parrot' sketch. Other Pythons are dressed as characters they are best remembered for – Idle's smarmy presenter, Palin's caricature northerner, Chapman's stiff-upper-lip military officer and Jones as a squawking, down-trodden housewife, a role he reprised as Brian's mother in *Life of Brian*. Gilliam, an American in the otherwise all-British troupe, was responsible for the surreal cartoon graphics that adorned *Monty Python's Flying Circus*. The show ran for five years from 1969 to 1974, changing the face of comedy with its absurdist sense of humour.

Life of Brian caused an enormous stir when it was first released in 1979. It was condemned as blasphemous, mainly by people who had not seen it, and banned in some towns and countries. But eventually it won (almost) universal acclaim for being a very funny film. Graham Chapman, who played Brian, died in 1989.

INDEX

PICTURE ACKNOWLEDGEMENTS

Abbreviations: t = top; m = middle; b = bottom; r = right; c = centre; l = left
All images in this book are courtesy of Getty Images, including the following which have additional attributions:

2-3, 143, 145: Time & Life Pictures
10-11, 98, 103, 104bl: Redferns/
  Virginia Turbett
20, 38, 39, 44r, 51, 56, 60, 82, 86,
  94b, 108, 118, 126, 133b, 140b:
  Popperfoto
22b, 25bl, 25br: Redferns/Tony Russell
24, 25t, 67, 71: Redferns/David Redfern
57: AFP
61: Redferns/GAB Archive

66, 70: Redferns/Ron Howard
68: Redferns/Ian Dickson
69: Redferns/Brian Cooke
72, 73: Anwar Hussein
83t: Robert Golden
88, 101: Redferns/Erica Echenberg
90: Redferns/Jan Persson
97: Redferns/Richard E Aaron
100: Redferns/Val Wilmer
102: Redferns/Jorgen Angel

104tl: Redferns/Peter Noble
104tr: Redferns/Rob Verhorst
105b: Sony Music Archive/Tom Sheehan
111, 114: Alex Bowie
117: Redferns/David Corio
119: Nobby Clark
122: John Downing
134b: CBS Photo Archive
134t: Michael Ochs Archive
137, 140t: Bob Thomas Sports

LOOKING BACK AT BRITAIN
FLOWER POWER TO UNION POWER – 1970s

Published in 2010 in the United Kingdom by
Vivat Direct Limited (t/a Reader's Digest) in association
with Getty Images and Endeavour London Limited

Vivat Direct Limited
(t/a Reader's Digest)
157 Edgware Road
London W2 2HR

Endeavour London Limited
21–31 Woodfield Road
London W9 2BA
info@endeavourlondon.com

Colour origination by Chroma Graphics Ltd, Singapore
Printed and bound in Europe by Arvato Iberia

For Endeavour
Publisher: Charles Merullo
Designer: Tea Aganovic
Picture editors: Jennifer Jeffrey, Franziska Payer Crockett
Production: Mary Osborne

For Vivat Direct (t/a Reader's Digest)
Editorial director: Julian Browne
Art director: Anne-Marie Bulat
Project editor: Christine Noble
Art editor: Conorde Clarke
Indexer: Marie Lorimer
Proofreader: Ron Pankhurst
Pre-press technical manager: Dean Russell
Product production manager: Claudette Bramble
Production controller: Sandra Fuller

Written by
James Harpur

CONCEPT CODE: UK 0154/L/S
BOOK CODE: 638-013 UP0000-1
ISBN: 978 0 276 44401 2
ORACLE CODE: 356900013H.00.24